A BOOK OF RITUALS

VOLUME 1

MOON MAGIC

A Lunar Guide to Achieving Goals
Without Burnout

By Melissa Lyon West

AWAKENED WITCH
PUBLISHING
SALT LAKE CITY

The mission of Awakened Witch Publishing is to provide inspiring works that empower women to connect with nature, discover their inner power, and live a magical life.

ISBN 9798991117104 (print) ISBN 9798991117128 (ebook)

To the witches in The Coaching Coven.
You are the magic.

I have found a way to be whole,
To be both fire and water,
To burn bright, then rest in the cool embrace
Of my own stillness.

There is a time for every part of me,
A rhythm that honors my pulse,
A dance where I lead and follow,
Where I rise and retreat,
Each in its own sacred turn.

I no longer fear my ambition,
No longer hide from my need to rest.
I have learned to carry both,
Like the moon holds light and shadow,
Balanced, complete.

In the quiet of the night,
I feel the deep relief
Of being fully seen,
Fully known,
By the cycles that cradle me,
By the self I have become.

In this embrace of all that I am,
I find my power,
My peace,
And the gentle ease
Of living true to my own design.

TABLE OF CONTENTS

TABLE OF CONTENTS

I'm so glad
you are here

hello!

Hey Sister,

Welcome to *Moon Magic,* the first volume in the *Book of Rituals* series. I've created this book, not as more work or another thing for you to do, but to inspire you to uncover the magic in everyday life and find the power that is already inside of you.

This book? It's like a worn, cherished journal—a collection of spells, musings, and whispered secrets meant for you. It's not just a book; it's an invitation to step into a world where building dreams meets everyday ease and joy.

Imagine this book as a nudge to explore your desires, emotions, and dreams. It's about empowering you to craft *your own* rituals, embrace your intentions, and sprinkle a bit of wonder into your life as you pursue your goals.

This isn't a roadmap - it's a compass. My hope is that as you immerse yourself in these pages, you find clarity, courage, growth, and a way to calm the chaos.

So here's to you—unveiling layers, seeking truths, and crafting rituals that speak to your heart as you embrace the beauty of your own story and connect to the moon's gentle rhythm.

I love you,

Melissa

INTRODUCTION

Let's start at the beginning. I was born and raised in a high-demand religion that celebrated male power and functioned through manipulation and control. I spent the first thirty years a prisoner in my own body, afraid of being seen and heard. I was in a constant state of fear, shame, and guilt.

I felt as if I had no voice. I did not know myself and had no deep friendships, or any real friendships at all. Ashamed of who I was and disconnected from my body, I kept my true self hidden.

Anxiety, panic attacks, depression... all hidden behind a smile.

I went to bed each night desperately wanting a bigger life, but knowing I wasn't good enough, I hadn't made enough progress. Tomorrow I would try harder...

After my third daughter was born, I was diagnosed with Lyme Disease, which sent me into one of the darkest periods of my life. It was in this darkness that the pressure of living up to perfection took its toll, and I hit rock bottom—causing cracks to form all over my perfectly plated life.

In this darkness, hope showed up. A woman befriended me—she was fire in human form. She was all the things I wasn't supposed to be.
She said and did whatever she wanted! She talked about her story vulnerably and without shame. Who was this magical person!?

Over the next few years, she helped me find my voice, courage, and bravery!

I made a decision during that time that changed my life...

No more lying.

No more pretending I was ok, pretending I was happy. No more pretending I didn't have questions and doubts.

This one decision caused me to practice courage daily. Slowly I left the rules that were crushing me. I started to see myself as worthy of my own love and acceptance, learned to see the divine inside my soul, and started to have fun for the first time in my life. I was learning to write my own rules, use my own voice, access my own power.

FREEDOM BEGAN TO BEAT IN MY CHEST!

It was at that point I found my soul's calling—to help women break out of their own prison of fear and discover the freedom to live a life they desired. For me, that most aligned with feelings-based, heart-centered life coaching. So, I went back to school, got my life coaching certificate, and started my business.

For years, I coached women who wanted more. They wanted to fall in love with themselves and leave behind toxic relationships, to launch businesses and find confidence to speak their truth, to live authentically and find the bravery to do so. I had the unique opportunity to work with these brave women to figure out what they truly wanted and walk with them toward that goal. I loved my work... But something was missing, and I couldn't quite put my finger on what it was.

So after the most successful spring in my business, I shut it all down.

I cocooned, I cried, and with the help of plant medicine, I did some deep healing.

Then, one day I woke up and remembered... I am a witch! You could see it all over my house—the jars of dried herbs, the crystals scattered on every surface, the tinctures and oils, the tarot and oracle cards stacked on my desk.

I am a woman who knows her power, a woman connected to nature, and that, that was the missing part. It was a new kind of freedom to fully embrace this part of me. The plants, the herbs, the tinctures, the crystals, and spells... They fit seamlessly with my love of coaching and building a life that brings joy to women.

So one day I sat down, and within four hours, I had created The Coaching Coven, a group coaching and online community for women. A week later, this book was born.

I combined what I know from coaching, what I learned from working with women who were working towards big goals, and what I love about witchcraft. What I quickly realized was that community, ritual, and cycles were at the heart of it all!

I started to develop the witch's way of avoiding burnout and I believe these three pieces can fundamentally change the way women move through life.

My goal with this book is for you to find more ease, joy, freedom, and fun as you work toward the big dreams you have inside your heart. To provide you a guide that offers a sustainable way to build a life of passion and purpose. This book pulls from wisdom from the wise women before us, the brave women today, and the message burning in my heart—we are better together, and we are more grounded connected to nature.

My work and the words in this book are all based on the following three concepts:

Community - Healing, growth, and self-care all happen with the support of others. Leaning into the truth that we are stronger together, women supporting women is the future.

Ritual - Aligning what you truly want in life with consistent, conscious, and meaningful routines transforms the mundane into the sacred, creating a life that feels rich and fulfilling.

Cycles - The moon has always had a very important place in witchcraft and a woman's life. By allowing time to grow, release, and rest, we are rejecting the systems that oppress us and remembering what our bodies have know all along—the magic is in us and all around us!

My hope is that this book will help you understand the energy of the moon, the power of ritual, and the fun of witchcraft to help you create a life that makes you excited to wake up in the morning, nourishes you when you are tired, and helps you learn to live a life of ease and magic.

THE BUILDING BLOCKS

This section explains why ritual and cycles are the foundation to achieving your goals without burnout. You will also learn how to set up a space to hold your rituals, how to use spell casting to reach your goals and live a magical life, and how to follow your own cycle for a more easeful life.

chapter one

THE FOUNDATION

laying the groundwork

UNDERSTANDING THE
MOON CYCLE

NEW MOON

WAXING CRESCENT

1ST QUARTER

WAXING GIBBOUS

FULL MOON

WANING GIBBOUS

3RD QUARTER

WANING CRESCENT

NEW MOON
set intentions
When the New Moon appears, listen to your intuition, determine what you want to nurture, and grow during this upcoming lunar phase.
This is a time for planting seeds.

WAXING CRESCENT
be curious
Embrace the excitement of new possibilities.
Use this time to explore, open your mind, and welcome the potential that lies ahead.

FIRST QUARTER
develop your intentions
Take action, laying the groundwork for your goals, and start building momentum.
This time is about putting plans into motion.

WAXING GIBBOUS
refine and take action
Refine your strategies, make adjustments, and focus on enhancements.
This phase encourages you to take deliberate action.

FULL MOON
celebrate your progress
Recognize how far you've come and revel in your achievements.
Release what no longer serves you.
It's a time for acknowledgment, gratitude, and release.

WANING GIBBOUS
complete and reflect
Wrap up actions and projects you started in the last few weeks; reflect on goal progress and lessons. Consider how you can share ideas and knowledge with others.
This phase is about reflection and giving back.

THIRD QUARTER
release
Take stock of your goal and intentions, identify what you can let go of, and create space for new beginnings.
It's a period of clearing and making room for growth.

WANING CRESCENT
embrace silence
Rest and restore, reconnect with your intuition.
It's a time for inner reflection and rejuvenation.

EMBRACE THE CYCLE,
FIND RENEWAL

Do you ever feel like time is slipping through your fingers? Like you are always behind in the day and in life? That you are running out of time?

We have been taught to think of life as a race against the clock, and it leaves us feeling rushed, exhausted, and disappointed in ourselves.

But here within these pages, we will learn from the ancient wisdom of witchcraft, feminine wisdom, and Mother Nature herself to see a way forward that offers ease, rest, and growth. A way to step outside of the systems that stole the knowledge and wisdom from us, to leave behind the systems that are making us sick and exhausted.

Instead of looking at time as a straight line, what would happen if you began to picture time as a circle—always coming back around. In that loop, there is room for us to refresh, grow, simply be, and *enjoy* our life.

Nature has handed us this magical reset button within its cycles, inviting us to find peace in that constant renewal—we now have the work of relearning what was hidden for so long.

The easiest way to picture time as a circle is to think of the seasons—spring with its new beginnings, summer full of growth and thriving, autumn shedding the old, and winter taking time to rest and retreat. But when you get to winter, it doesn't end, does it? No! It all comes back around again and again, a never-ending cycle of renewal.

Everywhere you look in nature, you will see cycles in motion, including the moon! The New Moon signals a fresh start. Then, it grows big and bright, shedding light on our achievements and motivating us to be seen.

Then, it gracefully lets go, encouraging us, to let go of what doesn't serve us before it drops into darkness to offer rest, and then back around to give a whole new opportunity for new beginnings.

Even our own bodies have a circular pattern! We go through stages of growth, peak, release, and rest. Just like how nature transitions from spring to summer, autumn to winter, our bodies follow this cyclical pattern, a constant reminder of renewal and transformation.

Time is not a stressful straight line we make it out to be. It is a circle, always giving us a chance for a restart. Every day is not a countdown.

We're not racing against a ticking clock; we are simply circling back for another round.

In this cycle, there's no loss—simply more opportunities to grow, create, release and rest.

I want to repeat this thought because it has the potential to release so much weight off your shoulders. **We are never running out of time; rather, we are always returning to a fresh start.**

Write it down and paste it to your mirror if you need to because this is a foundational thought that we will build off of in this book.

In a culture that has trained us to focus on hustle, constant forward motion, and a fear of running out of time, we will return to our bodies and the moon shining down on us. We will return to cyclical living, and this will make all the difference.

WHY DO WE NEED RITUAL?

Essentially, rituals create a sense of order, control, and relaxation in our lives, which can significantly contribute to our overall happiness and help calm the nervous system amidst life's challenges.

Rituals serve as profound anchors in the ebb and flow of our lives, connecting us to the cycles of nature and offering a sanctuary for our spirits when life is overwhelming. There are three main ways rituals do this:

- **Provide Predictability and Stability:** Rituals provide a sense of structure and predictability in our lives. When we engage in consistent habits, our brains register a pattern, reducing uncertainty and anxiety. This stability helps in calming the nervous system by offering a reliable framework that our minds and bodies can count on.

  - **Offer a Sense of Control:** Rituals give us a feeling of control in an often unpredictable world. By engaging in habits, we establish a routine that we have influence over, which can alleviate feelings of powerlessness. This control can help in reducing stress and promoting a sense of empowerment, contributing to a more positive emotional state.

  - **Trigger Relaxation Responses:** Certain rituals, especially those focused on relaxation or mindfulness (like meditation, deep breathing exercises, or bedtime routines), activate the parasympathetic nervous system. These activities promote relaxation and help in counteracting the effects of stress, leading to increased feelings of happiness and calmness.

THE MAGIC BEHIND BUILDING LASTING RITUALS

Habits form the cornerstone of our daily routines, saving our brains from the impossible task of making every choice consciously. Almost half (47%) of our daily decisions are habitual.

To understand how to actually create and form rituals that last longer than a few days, let's look at the research in behavioral psychology that points to the cue-habit-reward loop as a fundamental aspect of habit formation.

When you understand the science behind habit creation, it can empower you to establish enduring rituals that enhance your life.

The Cue-Habit-Reward Loop

- **Cue:** Cues act as triggers prompting habitual behavior. They can be external stimuli or internal mental prompts. For instance, the time of day, a specific location, or an emotional state can serve as cues.

- **Habit:** Habits are the actions we instinctively perform in response to cues. Repeated behaviors become ingrained habits stored in our subconscious.

- **Reward:** Rewards are the positive reinforcements linked to habits. They reinforce the behavior, making it more likely to recur in the future.

19

Hacking the Habit Loop

Understanding this loop allows us to strategically incorporate new habits into our lives. By understanding, manipulating, and piggybacking on existing cues, habits become malleable, allowing for intentional habit adjustments and the formation of lasting rituals.

For instance: Identify an existing daily cue, like drinking morning coffee, and associate a new habit, such as journaling, directly after it. Over time, the established cue triggers the desired habit.

SLOW & STEADY
Consistency is key!
Repeating the cue-habit-reward loop strengthens the neural pathways associated with the habit, making it automatic.

Aligning ritual with moon cycles allows us to benefit from the powerful energy that is pulsing through the universe and our own bodies. **In the midst of the chaos and burnout woven into the fabric of patriarchal systems, rituals become sanctuaries of self-care and resilience.** They provide moments of stillness, grounding us in the feminine energy that is often overlooked.

In doing so, we find solace, rejuvenation, and a source of empowerment, pushing back against the relentless pace of a society that disregards the restorative power of sacred pauses.

CUE-ACTION-REWARD

**These examples show how using already established cues
can make adding new rituals much easier.**

- Breathwork
  - Cue: Taking a shower
  - Action: Focused breathing and visualization
  - Reward: Feeling energized or relaxed and accomplished, releasing endorphins

- Gratitude Journaling
  - Cue: Sitting down with a cup of tea in the evening
  - Action: Writing three things you're grateful for
  - Reward: Fostering a sense of positivity and contentment before bed

- Visualization Practice
  - Cue: Before starting work or a project
  - Action: Spending five minutes visualizing achieving the goal
  - Reward: Increased motivation, clarity, and focus on the desired outcome

- Evening Self-Reflection
  - Cue: Dimming the lights before bed
  - Action: Reflecting on the day's achievements and areas for change
  - Reward: A sense of closure, learning from the day, and setting intentions for tomorrow

- Nature Walk Routine
  - Cue: Finishing morning coffee
  - Action: Taking a 20-minute walk
  - Reward: Refreshed mind, increased creativity, and improved mood from exposure to natural surroundings

CREATING A SACRED SPACE

Designing a sacred space is a tender act of creating a haven—
a place where the outside world fades and you can focus on your
goal, magic, and rituals.

It's not just about your physical surroundings; it's crafting an
atmosphere that resonates with you and feels safe and magical.

Here's How to Create a Sacred Space:

- Begin by selecting a space, such as a little corner, desk, shelf, or an entire room. As a practical rule of thumb, choose a space in your bedroom. It will give you the privacy needed to do your rituals, and it's usually where you feel safest.

- Next, declutter and clean the area—remove everything from the space and wipe down the space, clearing and washing away stagnant energy. As you cleanse, let go of any stress or negativity, inviting in fresh, positive vibrations.

- Then, create your altar, or sacred space. Crafting your altar is a deeply personal journey, an artistic expression of your inner world. Add in candles, crystals, dried flowers, plants, photos, personal mementos— choose things that make you smile, feel grounded, or hold special meaning.

Remember, it's not about what others consider traditional or magical; it's about what resonates deeply within you. Your space is a reflection of your journey and will grow and shift over time. It is a space where you find solace, power, and focus during your rituals.

Trust your intuition, and let your creativity shape the space that speaks to your soul.

22

WHAT IS SPELL CASTING?

Spell casting is the practice of using rituals, incantations, gestures, or tools to channel and direct energy to align with your desires. It's a form of focused intention that aims to bring about a specific outcome or change in your life, environment, or circumstances.

At its core, spellwork revolves around the belief that energy can be manipulated and directed to influence events or manifest desires. Spells can take various forms, from simple affirmations or prayers to more elaborate rituals involving candles, herbs, crystals, or symbolic objects.

The process typically involves setting a clear intention, raising and focusing energy, and then releasing it into the universe to bring about the desired result.

Ultimately, spell casting is a tool for you to connect with your intentions, tap into your inner power, and create positive changes in alignment with your desires and beliefs.

SPELL WORK BASICS

The New Moon phase lasts for about three days, offering a brief yet potent window for setting intentions and planting the seeds of your dreams. This is a time for new beginnings, reflection, and aligning your energy with your deepest desires. Embrace this period to envision the future you wish to create.

Moon Energy

Working with the moon's phases makes spells stronger. When you align your spells with the moon's rhythms, you tap into powerful cosmic forces, making your magic more effective. Our magic is stronger when we connect with the moon!

Intention is Key

At the core of every spell lies intention. Your intention is the thought that helps you focus on making your dreams a reality. Clarifying your intent is the cornerstone of effective magic work. By focusing on what you truly desire, you give your magic a precise direction, ensuring that your actions are aligned with your goal.

Harnessing Energy

Spells tap into the energy of the universe. Whether it's through visualization, meditation, or rituals, directing and manipulating this energy is central to casting successful spells.

Tools as Amplifiers

Crystals, candles, herbs, and symbols—these are tools that act as conduits, amplifying your intentions and aiding in focusing your mind and energy during your spellwork.

Mindfulness and Presence

The state of mind during spell casting is crucial. Being present, focused, and mindful allows for a deeper connection to the intention being set. It involves immersing oneself fully in the ritual or practice, bringing heightened awareness to the moment of casting.

Release and Surrender

A fundamental aspect of spell casting involves releasing the intention into the universe. After focusing and directing energy toward the desired outcome, the final step is surrendering the spell's energy, allowing it to manifest without attachment or doubt.

Spell work can be a powerful way to achieve your goals as it helps you focus your energy and intentions on what you truly want. By casting a spell, you bring yourself into the present moment, making your desires feel more real and attainable. It's a fun and creative process that allows you to connect with your inner magic, turning your goals into reality while enjoying the journey.

HARNESSING MOON PHASES
FOR SPELL WORK

  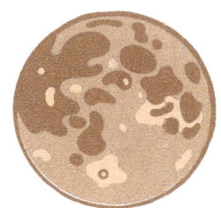  

Aligning your spell work with the moon phases can enhance the effectiveness and potency of your intentions. However, your intuition and personal connection to the moon's energies are equally essential.

Experiment with different phases and observe how their energies resonate with your desires and spell work.

New Moon
- Intentions: Ideal for setting new intentions, starting projects, or planting seeds for new beginnings. Spells related to manifestation, goal-setting, and initiating change are potent during this phase.

Waxing Crescent
- Growth and Expansion: Use this phase to amplify intentions set during the New Moon. Spells focused on growth, development, and bringing intentions to fruition are most effective now.

Waxing Gibbous
- Refinement and Adjustment: Perfect for fine-tuning, refining, and adjusting goals. Spells aimed at tweaking plans or removing obstacles hindering progress align well with this phase.

Full Moon
- Culmination and Power: The Full Moon is a potent time for maximum energy and manifestation. Spells focused on fruition, completion, and powerful manifestations are best cast during this phase.

Waning Gibbous
- Release and Letting Go: Utilize this phase for releasing negativity, breaking bad habits, or letting go of what no longer serves you. Spells related to cleansing, banishing, and releasing are effective now.

Waning Crescent
- Rest and Renewal: This phase is a time for rest, introspection, and preparing for the new cycle. Use this phase for deep inner work, meditation, and spiritual renewal.

THIS FEELS LIKE A GOOD TIME TO TELL YOU...

I do not do all the things in this book every cycle. Sometimes I rush when I should rest and skip rituals, even though I know they would help me. But remember, this is a cycle. It will come around again, and that is a witch's biggest secret. I don't need to stress or try to be perfect because I am learning and evolving each month.

Each phase will cycle around again, and I will know a little more. I will be myself a little more. I am human. I am growing. I am not just connected to nature, I am nature. You and I don't need to seek perfection because our learning, growing, and evolving is perfect.

CRAFTING PERSONALIZED SPELLS & AFFIRMATIONS

Crafting your own spells or affirmations is a powerful way to align your energy with your goals and desires. Explore your creativity and intentions to create personalized spells that resonate deeply with you.

Steps to Crafting Spells or Affirmations

1. **Define Your Intention:** Clarify your goal or desire. What do you need to manifest or change in your life? Be specific and clear in articulating your intention.
2. **Create Emotional Alignment:** Consider the emotions associated with your intention. What feelings do you wish to cultivate or release? Infuse your spells with these emotions.
3. **Craft Your Spell or Affirmation:** Write down phrases or sentences that encapsulate your intention. Let them be concise, affirmative, and emotionally charged.
4. **Incorporate Symbolic Tools**: Use elements like candles, crystals, or herbs that resonate with your intention. These tools combine with your inner power to amplify your intention. See Chapter 10 for a brief guide on which herbs, crystals, and colors to use in your spells.
5. **Infuse Personal Energy:** Consider how you will infuse your words with personal energy, intention, and belief. Your energy is a vital component of the effectiveness of your spells.

LET IT BE FUN!

In a world often driven by productivity and external validation, the notion of pleasure—particularly for women—has been caught in a complex web of societal expectations. The demands of the patriarchy and capitalism have sculpted a narrative that downplays and shames the pursuit of pleasure and fun for women.

Yet, the essence of pleasure isn't frivolous; it's an integral part of our mental and emotional well-being. The science behind pleasure illuminates its profound impact on mental health. Neurologically, pleasure stimulates the release of neurotransmitters like dopamine and endorphins, fostering feelings of happiness, reducing stress, and enhancing overall well-being.

Societal and religious teachings frequently misinterpret pleasure as indulgence, often labeling it as unwarranted or selfish. But to be honest, acknowledging the necessity to change this outdated narrative is much simpler than actually fully accepting that prioritizing self-pleasure, play, and fun is an expression of self-love and pivotal for mental health.

To truly shift these ingrained societal norms, we have to actively engage in pleasure and play and then confront any feelings of guilt or shame that arise. This process involves taking concrete steps towards embracing a fresh perspective, one that prioritizes physical well-being and recognizes the profound role of pleasure in nurturing mental and emotional strength. It's a journey towards adopting a mindset that values play and champions the significance of pleasure in cultivating resilience—one thought, one action at a time.

So let these rituals, spells, and ideas be your permission slip to have fun and play! If it begins to feel hard or makes you feel guilty for "doing it wrong," take a breath and remember that YOU are the magic. This journey is here to add ease, not stress! So dance a little dance, take a nap, drink some water... and know that fresh starts are always there waiting for you.

HONORING YOUR UNIQUE CYCLE

If you bleed, by syncing your rituals with your menstrual cycle instead of the moon, you honor your body's natural rhythms. This personalized approach helps you work with your creativity, drive, and need for rest, offering relief and allowing you to move in harmony with your body. **This approach helps prevent burnout as you begin to work with your body and not against it!**

How to apply *Moon Magic* to your own cycle:

The New Moon - Planting Seeds - Menstrual Phase
This is a time of rest and reflection. As your period wanes, focus on setting intentions and planting seeds for what you want to grow in the upcoming cycle.

Waxing Crescent - Possibilities and Potential
Follicular phase, the 5-7 days following your bleed
This is a time of renewed energy and creativity. Explore new ideas and start taking steps toward your goals.

Waxing Gibbous - Aligned Action
Follicular phase, the 5-7 days before ovulation
Your energy continues to build. Focus on aligned action and fine-tuning your plans as you prepare for the peak of your cycle.

The Full Moon - Celebrate and Release
Ovulation (Around the middle of your cycle, typically 2-3 days)
This is a time of celebration and release. Celebrate your achievements, and release any tension or emotions that no longer serve you.

The Waning Gibbous - Sacred Release
Luteal Phase, the 5-7 days after ovulation
As your energy begins to wane, release what's no longer needed.

The Waning Crescent - Nurturing Self
Luteal Phase leading into Menstruation (5-7 days before your period starts)
Your energy is low, making it a perfect time for self-care and nurturing. Prepare to enter the next cycle by resting and taking care of yourself.

ACTION STEPS

This book is only as good as the time and effort you put into follow-through! It is designed to take you one simple step at a time. There is no time limit. Simply do what you can when you can.

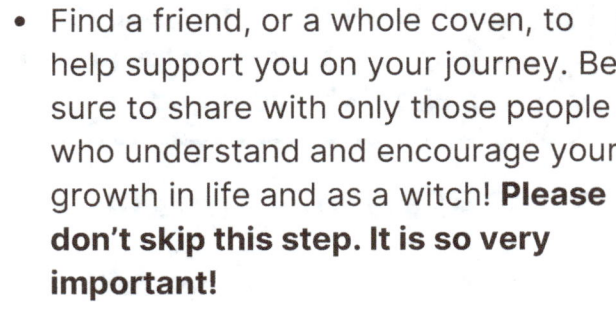

- Find a friend, or a whole coven, to help support you on your journey. Be sure to share with only those people who understand and encourage your growth in life and as a witch! **Please don't skip this step. It is so very important!**

- Create your sacred space! This is such a fun and exciting time as you start your journey. Share pictures with your support network.

- Take 20-30 minutes to reflect on what you learned on the following page. Journaling pages are easy to skip over. You might think you will come back or maybe you just want to get on with the REAL work. But slow down -- *this is the real work*!

- Find some time on your calendar and schedule yourself time to read, journal, or practice spell work. Make it reoccurring and treat it like it's actually important. Because you are worthy of alone time... I promise!

When I reflect on my current connection to the Moon and her cycles, how does it influence my life, if at all?

What am I most hoping to get out of this book?

Do I feel any resistance or skepticism around the idea of sacred space? Where do I think this resistance stems from?

What part of this journey am I most excited about?

awaken the witch within

WHAT DO YOU REALLY WANT?

We bring things into our life when we focus our energy on that thing. The New Moon is a dark and inward energy. A time to imagine what you truly want and plant that seed in the dark earth. Over the next month, that idea will grow and flourish.

chapter two

THE NEW MOON

a 2-3 day phase for new beginnings

35

OH, THIS IS MAGICAL!

After realizing the wisdom of returning to nature's cycles and the power of ritual, I began seeing the New Moon as a powerful reminder to pause and set my intentions for the coming cycle. Each New Moon, I dedicated time to holding a personal ritual—a sacred pause amidst the chaos of daily life as an ambitious entrepreneur, mom, wife, and friend.

This ritual wasn't just about setting goals; it was about being in the feelings of my dreams without the need to hustle. I began to believe I didn't have to work so hard to create a life I loved. I could use my magic to see a path forward, trusting the Universe to help make it happen.

This pause allowed me to make a day that was previously overlooked into a whole moment. It turned into a ritual that made me feel enchanted and magical. I would clean and refresh my sacred space, light a candle, take a deep breath, play with crystals, herbs, and candles and feel into what I wanted to see happen that cycle.

Here's what that looked like while I was writing this book:
On the New Moon, I focused on my main goal: "Release *Moon Magic* in October 2024, trusting it will inspire and empower those who are meant to find it." I then decided what was reasonable to accomplish in the next three weeks, such as finishing the second draft and seeking feedback from advanced readers.

I wrote my intention in an uplifting way, such as, "As I complete this second draft, I release perfectionism and embrace sharing with my readers, trusting their feedback will amplify its power and impact." I could infuse the intention with gratitude, place it somewhere visible, or seal it in a vial with herbs and crystals until the Full Moon.

This practice clarified my desires, aligned them with my heart, and created a solid road map for the coming moon cycle.

This ritual became a cornerstone of my creative process, not just for writing, but for all areas of my life. It was a way to reconnect with my feminine wisdom and the natural cycles that govern so much of our lives, whether we realize it or not. As I continued to honor the New Moon, I noticed a shift in how I approached my work and my personal life. Instead of feeling overwhelmed by the demands of my roles, I felt more grounded and in control.

The New Moon intention setting ritual became a touchstone—a reminder that I could slow down, reflect, and realign with my true intentions every single cycle.

This practice of tuning in to my own rhythms and the lunar cycle helped me avoid burnout, keeping me balanced and energized for the long haul. Incorporating this approach into my life transformed the way I achieved my goals. I no longer felt the constant pressure to be in "go mode" all the time. Instead, I learned to trust in the ebb and flow of energy.

Through these rituals, I realized that magic isn't just about casting spells or making things happen instantly. **It's about being present, intentional, and aligned with the natural rhythms of the world around us.** By syncing my life with the moon's phases, I found a deeper sense of purpose and peace. I began to see that I was co-creating my reality with the Universe, and that I could do so with ease—something I desperately needed!

As you consider your own goals and dreams, allow yourself to pause, reflect, and set intentions with each New Moon. Create your own rituals that feel magical and meaningful to you. Whether it's lighting a candle, writing in a journal, or simply taking a few moments of quiet reflection, these small acts can have a profound impact on how you move through your life.

Embrace the power of ritual and the wisdom of nature's cycles, and watch as your life begins to align in beautiful, unexpected ways.

NEW MOON ENERGY

The New Moon phase lasts for about three days, offering a brief yet potent window for setting intentions and planting the seeds of your dreams. This is a time for new beginnings, reflection, and aligning your energy with your deepest desires. Embrace this period to envision the future you wish to create.

Go Inward

The New Moon arrives, not visible in the sky—a chance to reset, recharge, and dream anew. Its energy is quiet, offering an invitation to go inward and reflect on your desires.

Tip: Take a deep breath. No matter what happened last cycle, nature is offering you a fresh start.

Reflect

Take this time to delve deep within. Reflect on your aspirations, desires, and dreams. What do you wish to manifest in your life? What goals align with your heart's true desires? What do you want to cultivate during this moon cycle?

Tip: Reflect on your goal to identify the next best step to move forward.

Align

The dark moon invites us to focus our energies on our own reset. Embrace its potential energy to sow new dreams and establish intentions.

Tip: Don't feel like you have to do it all. Identify one key area to focus on and cultivate during this moon cycle.

Set Intentions

Harness the power of the New Moon by setting an intention aligned with your goal. Craft your intention with clarity and specificity. Visualize it as already achieved, infusing the words with emotion and conviction.

Tip: Write your intention for the cycle by clearly stating what you want to achieve. Be specific, positive, and heartfelt.

Ritual

Create a personal ritual to solidify your intentions. Light a candle, breathe deeply, and speak your goals aloud. Write them down, infuse them with gratitude, and place them where you can revisit them regularly.

Tip: Creating a New Moon ritual has no set rules. This is a place to try new things and see what feels good to you!

Accept the Journey

Remember, the New Moon isn't just about setting goals—it's about embarking on a transformative journey. There is no right or wrong here. Do what feels good and embrace the process. Remain open to the opportunities and ideas that come up.

Tip: Allow this process to be relaxing. Remember, have fun while learning, allowing your journey to unfold naturally and joyfully.

Live in the Now

The New Moon offers a powerful opportunity to pause, reset, and start fresh with your goals. Instead of constantly pushing forward and fixating on the future, use this time to create a ritual that anchors you in the present moment. By focusing on the present, you shift from a mindset of relentless striving to one of mindful presence. **Begin to appreciate the here and now so you can avoid burnout and find joy in the process.**

ACTION STEPS

By incorporating these action steps into your New Moon rituals and practices, you can harness the potent energy of the lunar cycle to clarify your intentions, align your focus, and take meaningful steps toward manifesting your goals and desires.

- **Set Clear Intentions:** Reflect on your goal. Define what you want to manifest or achieve during the upcoming lunar cycle.

- **Perform a New Moon Ritual:** This can include meditation, visualization, or casting a spell to cleanse and bless your space while setting intentions for the month ahead.

- **Create a Vision Board:** Use the New Moon energy to visualize your goals and dreams. Place this board in a prominent location where you can see it daily, reinforcing your intentions.

- **Establish a New Habit:** Identify a small, positive habit that supports your goals and start integrating it into your daily routine. This could be anything from spending a few minutes each day planning your tasks to practicing mindfulness or journaling about your progress.

I embrace my ability to create
anything I want in this life

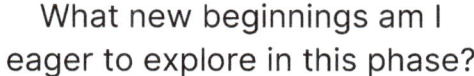

What new beginnings am I
eager to explore in this phase?

What intentions or
goals am I setting for
this lunar cycle?

What areas of my life need a
reset or a clean slate?

What dreams or desires am I
manifesting under the New Moon?

New Moon Notes

NEW MOON
SPELLS & RITUALS

I wrote these rituals and spells for myself as I work toward my own goals, and I am honored to share them with you. They are designed to help you focus your intentions, get clear on the path ahead, and align with the energy of new beginnings.

NEW MOON RITUAL

purpose: restart, plant new intentions
when to hold: the New Moon
ritual time: 30-45 minutes
Ingredients:

- white candles (for purification and clarity)
- incense, bell or smudge bundle (for cleansing and setting sacred space)
- paper and pen (for writing intentions)

HOW TO PERFORM:

- **Preparing**: Find a quiet and comfortable space. Light the incense or sage bundle to cleanse the area and yourself. Set up your ritual space with candles, crystals, and your journal.

- **Centering and Grounding:** Take a few deep breaths to center yourself. Imagine roots growing from your body into the ground, rooting you.

- **Candle Lighting:** Light the candles, symbolizing new beginnings and the start of the ritual.

- **Intention Setting**: Close your eyes and focus on your breath. Visualize what you want to manifest in the upcoming lunar cycle. Write down your intentions in your journal. Be specific, clear, and positive as if your desires have already come to fruition.

- **Affirming:** Speak your intentions aloud, affirming them with confidence and belief. For example: "I am open to receiving abundance" or "I am stepping into my personal power."

- **Releasing**: Choose a method that feels meaningful to you for releasing your intention into the New Moon's energy.
    - Planting: Bury in soil or a pot, symbolizing growth.
    - Burning: Safely burn the paper, symbolizing releasing your desire into the universe.
    - Placing Under Pillow/Mattress: Slip it beneath for subconscious integration during sleep.

- **Closing**: Express gratitude for the opportunities ahead. Thank the Universe, any guides, or deities you work with. Blow out the candles, symbolizing the end of the ritual.

Notes:

A MANIFESTATION SPELL

spell purpose: create custom vision board

when to cast: the New Moon

ritual time: 30-60 minutes

ingredients:
- white candle (for purification and clarity)
- free Canva account
- printer

HOW TO PERFORM:

- **Prepare**: Clear and ground into your space by lighting your candle. Take three deep, slow breaths. Read your goal out loud.
- **Get Clear:** Ask yourself these questions:
  - Imagine your dream scenario in 6 months. What does your life look like as you live in the reality of a successful goal?
  - How would it FEEL to live each day after achieving your goal? Use a feelings wheel (see Chapter 10) and get as specific as you can.
  - Now get even more specific! What kind of setting are you in? Who is in your life? What does it look, feel, taste, smell, and sound like to be living in that reality?
- **Feel:** Use Canva's search feature to find specific images, symbols, and words that align with your goal. Choose visuals that evoke the *feelings* you wish to manifest and create a vision board on Canva.
- **Focus:** Print your vision board and take a moment to focus your energy. Visualize a glowing light surrounding the page, infusing your creation with positive energy. Imagine the vision board being charged with the power of your intentions.
- **Chant (optional):** Speak your intention for the board out loud or use this spell:

  "Visions clear, dreams ignite,
  Universe, align with my heart's light.
  Manifest truth that I long to see,
  As I will, so shall it be."
- **Close**: Conclude the spell by extinguishing the candle and expressing gratitude. Thank the Universe or any higher power you believe in for assisting you in manifesting your desires.

NEW MOON BATH RITUAL

spell purpose: setting intentions and manifesting goals

when to cast: on the New Moon   **ritual time:** 30-40 minutes

ingredients: Epsom salts or bath crystals, essential oils (e.g., lavender, jasmine, frankincense), candle(s) for ambiance, small crystal (e.g., clear quartz, amethyst)

HOW TO PERFORM:

- **Prepare Your Bath:** Draw a warm bath and add oils, Epsom salts or bath crystals to the water.
- **Set the Mood:** Light candles around the bathroom to create a calming ambiance. Play soft music or nature sounds, if desired, to further enhance the atmosphere.
- **Enter with Intentions:** Before stepping into the bath, close your eyes and set your intentions for the New Moon cycle. Visualize your goals as already accomplished and feel the emotions associated with success.
- **Immerse Yourself:** Step into the bath mindfully, allowing the warm water to envelop your body. Relax and let go of any tension or stress as you soak in the rejuvenating water.
- **Connect with Lunar Energy:** Hold a small crystal (e.g., clear quartz, amethyst) in your hands while soaking. Visualize the crystal absorbing the cleansing and manifesting the energy of the New Moon.
- **Repeat Affirmations:** While in the bath, speak affirmations related to your intentions aloud or silently. Examples of affirmations: "I am worthy of rest" or "My creative spirit is awakening."
- **Release and Let Go:** Imagine any doubts or obstacles dissolving and washing away with the bathwater. Trust in the process of manifestation and surrender to the Universe's guidance.
- **Express gratitude:** Thank the Universe for its support in manifesting your desires.
- **Close the Ritual:** When you're ready to leave the bath, visualize your intentions firmly anchored within you. Step out of the bath feeling renewed, empowered, and aligned with your goals.

SACRED SPACE CLEANSING SPELL

spell purpose: clean your sacred space and infuse with new intentions

when to cast: on the New Moon   **ritual time:** 30-40 minutes

ingredients: • smudge bundle, incense, Palo Santo stick, or bell
- bowl of saltwater
- clean cloth or sponge
- white candle (symbolizes purity and illumination)
- small bowl of dried herbs (such as lavender or sage)

HOW TO PERFORM:

- **Prepare Your Space:** Begin by tidying up your sacred space, removing any clutter or unnecessary items. Open a window or door to allow fresh air to circulate.
- **Clear Negative Energy:** Light the white candle in the center of your space. Light the smudge bundle or incense. Starting from the entrance, walk clockwise around the room, gently waving the smoke into corners and along walls. Visualize the smoke clearing away any stagnant or negative energy, creating a clean and sacred atmosphere.
- **Wipe Down Surfaces:** Dip the clean cloth or sponge into the bowl of saltwater. Begin wiping down surfaces like altars, tables, and shelves. As you clean, envision the saltwater purifying and cleansing these spaces, preparing them for new energy and intentions.
- **Infuse with Blessing Herbs:** Take a pinch of the dried herbs from the bowl and sprinkle them around the room, focusing on areas that need extra blessings or attention. As you do this, recite a simple blessing or affirmation, such as:
    "With salt and herb, I cleanse and bless,
    Removing old to invite newness and success.
    May this space be pure and bright,
    Filled with love, joy, and positive light."
- **Set New Intentions:** Close your eyes and visualize your sacred space filled with the energy of your new intentions. Imagine what you wish to cultivate in this space— peace, creativity, inspiration, or spiritual connection.
- **Seal the Spell:** Thank the spirits or energies that assisted you during this cleansing and blessing. Blow out the candle, knowing that your sacred space is now purified, refreshed, and aligned with your renewed intentions.

Perform this spell each New Moon. Each time you clean and bless your space with intention, you reinforce its sacredness and invite positive energies into your life.

IDEAS BEGIN TO FLOW

As the moon starts to grow, the next week is all about the slow and steady starting of projects. Ideas will begin to flow; energy will pick up. There is no need to rush. If you have a day where you feel the need to go inward and rest, embrace it! Like a cold rainy day in spring, sometimes we just need to cuddle up with a book and know the sun and energy for garden work will be there tomorrow.

chapter three

THE WAXING CRESCENT MOON

a 5-7 day phase for possibilities and potential

THE SLOW AND STEADY BUILD

As the moon begins to grow, I embrace the Waxing Crescent as a time to slowly and steadily bring my intentions to life. This phase is about the gentle unfolding of new beginnings, where ideas start to flow, and energy begins to pick up. But just as a rainy spring day invites us to pause and rest, I remind myself that there's no need to rush. Some days, I may feel called to go inward, to recharge, and that's perfectly okay. **The energy to move forward will be there when I'm ready.**

During this phase, I start to see the first steps of my intentions come to life. It's a time for nurturing my ideas, allowing them to take root. I spend this week giving my projects gentle attention—writing out my ideas, planning, and envisioning what they could become—while also honoring the need to rest when necessary.

Here's what that looked like while I was writing this book:

After setting my intention to complete the second draft and ask for feedback from readers, I allowed the Waxing Crescent energy to guide my next steps. If one day I felt the urge to dive into writing, I followed that flow. But if another day called for rest and reflection, I embraced it, trusting that this balance would keep my creative energy alive. Instead, I would write down ideas, to-dos, and action steps that needed to be taken when my energy was ready for that. **This phase teaches us that growth doesn't always mean constant action; sometimes, it's about letting ideas incubate until they're ready to bloom.**

This gentle yet steady approach ensured that my actions aligned with my intuition and body, allowing me to move forward with purpose *and* ease. After experiencing burnout, this was key for me! By the end of the Waxing Crescent, I found myself not only making progress but also feeling energized and excited to ramp up my productivity and get my action list moving!

As the moon continues to grow, transitioning further into the Waxing Crescent phase, the energy around me begins to intensify, subtly but surely. This is the time when the initial seed of intention starts to evolve into something more tangible. The ideas that once floated like wisps of inspiration now begin to solidify, and with them comes a quiet but persistent drive to move forward.

During the Waxing Crescent, I find that my ideas start to take form, not in a rush, but with a steady, gentle pace. This is when I begin to flesh out concepts, explore possibilities, and let inspiration guide me without forcing it. It's a time for dreaming and envisioning what could be, while still allowing space for rest and reflection. The balance between action and rest is crucial here, as it prevents burnout and keeps my energy sustainable.

When I was writing this book, the Waxing Crescent phase was when I allowed myself time to brainstorm, outline, and explore new angles. I knew that each idea, whether it made it into the final draft or not, was a valuable part of the creative journey. The process was less about forcing progress and more about allowing the natural momentum to carry me forward. I didn't pressure myself to have everything figured out at once. Instead, I allowed myself to explore different possibilities, to play with ideas without the pressure of immediate execution.

This phase also taught me the importance of patience. There were days when inspiration flowed effortlessly, but there were also days when I felt the need to step back, to let the ideas settle and take shape on their own. **I learned to trust this ebb and flow, recognizing that progress isn't always linear but rather a dance between action and stillness.**

By the end of the Waxing Crescent, I had a clearer vision of my project and a growing excitement for that work ahead. The small, intentional steps I took during this phase laid a solid foundation for the work ahead, allowing me to build momentum without losing sight of my well-being. This approach not only made the process more enjoyable but also kept me connected to my creative energy in a sustainable way.

WAXING CRESCENT MOON ENERGY

The Waxing Crescent moon lasts for about a week, a gentle yet powerful time to nurture your intention. This is a period for gradual growth where ideas start to take shape. Embrace this phase to slowly and steadily bring your dreams to life, allowing your projects to unfold with patience and care, while also honoring any need for rest along the way.

Grow

The energy of the Waxing Crescent moon is all about possibilities and potential. It's a time when the energy begins to build, encouraging growth and forward momentum. Much like the vibrant energy of spring, this phase is perfect for initiating new projects and ideas.

Tip: Take one small, actionable step each day, such as organizing your thoughts, to help build momentum.

Reflect

Reflect on the intentions you set during the New Moon and consider the steps needed to achieve them. This phase invites you to think about the direction you want to take. Use this time to gain clarity about what needs to be done.

Tip: Start an idea list in your journal to keep track of your thoughts.

Set Intentions

The Waxing Crescent moon is a powerful time for setting the groundwork for future success. Focus on what you want to grow and manifest and outline the steps to get there.

Tip: Create a detailed action list of tasks that align with your goals. Take a moment to review the intentions you set during the New Moon. Break them down into smaller, manageable tasks that can be accomplished throughout the week.

Align

This is the ideal time to start moving toward your goals, making plans, and taking the first steps. Ensure your efforts are in harmony with the intentions you set during the New Moon.

Tip: Create a weekly action plan. Set aside specific times in your schedule for your action items, and commit to taking at least one concrete step each day.

Perform Rituals

Incorporating rituals into your goal-setting process helps anchor your intentions, transforming abstract ideas into tangible actions. By engaging in rituals, you create a sacred space that reinforces your commitment, aligns your energy with the waxing moon's growth, and fosters a deeper connection to the journey ahead.

Tip: Make space on your calendar and add your rituals to your schedule. Hold rituals that symbolize new beginnings and growth. Light a candle to represent the increasing light and energy of the moon. Write down your action steps on a piece of paper and keep it somewhere visible, or perform a simple ceremony to affirm your commitment to your goals.

Embrace Patience

Remember that this phase is the beginning of a journey. The Waxing Crescent moon encourages you to take small, steady steps toward your larger vision. Embrace the process, knowing that each step forward brings you closer to your dreams.

Tip: Celebrate small steps. At the end of each day or week, reflect on what you've accomplished and how it contributes to your overall goal.

ACTION STEPS

As the Waxing Crescent moon grows in the night sky, its energy supports new beginnings and the manifestation of your goals. This is a time to build momentum and start taking concrete steps toward your aspirations.

- **Make a List:** Write down a detailed list of tasks and steps needed to achieve your goals. Break them down into manageable actions you can start taking immediately.

- **Set Milestones:** Outline key milestones and deadlines for your goals. Identify the first few steps and set specific dates to accomplish them, helping you stay on track and maintain momentum.

- **Check In on Your New Habit:** Reflect on the habit you established during the New Moon phase. Assess how it's integrating into your routine and how it's impacting your progress. Make any necessary adjustments to ensure it continues to support your goals and a life of ease effectively.

- **Practice Meditation and Visualization:** Incorporate daily meditation and visualization practices to stay aligned with your intentions. Spend time each day visualizing yourself achieving your goals and feeling the emotions associated with success. See Chapter 9 for ideas.

I take things
one step at a time

What affirmations or mantras can I repeat to amplify my intentions?

In what ways am I adapting to new opportunities that have emerged?

How have my intentions from the New Moon begun to take shape?

What small steps or actions can I take to support my growing goals?

Waxing Crescent Moon Notes

WAXING CRESCENT MOON SPELLS & RITUALS

These spells are designed to help build confidence, momentum, and foster the conditions needed for growth and progress. The Waxing Crescent energy supports the gentle unfolding of your intentions, helping to bring them into reality without overwhelming you.

ENDURING AMBITION SPELL

spell purpose: steadiness in pursuing goals

when to cast: the Waxing Crescent or first quarter phase

ritual time: 10 minutes

ingredients:
- A candle (color of your choice)
- A small crystal or stone

HOW TO PERFORM:

- **Setup:** Sit comfortably and place the crystal in front of you.

- **Intentions:** Hold the crystal and focus on your goal. Envision yourself steadily progressing toward it, feeling determined and focused.

- **Charging the Crystal:** Pass the crystal over the flame of the candle, visualizing the candle's energy infusing into the crystal, imparting stability and determination.

- **Affirmation:** Repeat an affirmation aloud or in your mind, such as "With this crystal's steady might, I remain focused day and night."

- **Place the Crystal:** Set the crystal near your workspace or carry it with you (stick it in your bra next to your heart!) as a reminder of your steadfast pursuit of your goal.

- **Closing**: Conclude the spell by extinguishing the candle and expressing gratitude. Thank the Universe or any higher power you believe in for assisting you in manifesting your desires.

STEAMY IDEAS SPELL

spell purpose: clarity and ideas for a goal or task

when to cast: the Waxing Crescent or first quarter

ritual time: 10-15 minutes

ingredients:
- your favorite mug of hot tea or coffee
- pen and notebook

HOW TO PERFORM:

- **Set the Scene**: Find a peaceful spot and sit comfortably with a warm drink.
- **Meditate**: Close your eyes, take deep breaths, and focus on the rising steam. Envision the steam as a channel for clarity and focus.
- **Set Intentions**: Hold the mug and visualize your goals or tasks clearly. Imagine the warmth infusing you with determination and concentration.
- **Chant (optional)**: Whisper or think a personal affirmation while holding the mug, such as "With every sip, ideas flow and my goal will grow."
- **Sip Slowly:** Take deliberate sips, feeling the warmth spreading through your body and bringing focus and determination.
- **Journal**: Keep a notebook close by to write down your ideas. This allows your brain and energy to continue to flow without worrying about holding on to the ideas.
- **Close and Express Gratitude**: Conclude the spell by expressing gratitude to the Universe, yourself, or even the herbs and tea. Thank the Universe or any higher power you believe in for assisting you in manifesting your desires.

GENTLE PROGRESS RITUAL

spell purpose: to harness the gentle, building energy of the Waxing Crescent moon to achieve your goals with ease and flow

when to cast: the Waxing Crescent **ritual time:** 20-30 minutes

ingredients:
- white or green candle (for growth and new beginnings)
- small piece of paper and a pen
- sprig of rosemary or lavender (for clarity and calm)
- bowl of water (symbolizing flow and ease)

HOW TO PERFORM:

- **Set the Space:** Find a quiet place where you can sit comfortably. Light the candle in front of you, with the bowl of water to one side and the sprig of rosemary or lavender on the other. Take a few deep breaths, grounding yourself in the present moment.
- **Write Your Intentions:** On the piece of paper, write down your goals or intentions for this lunar cycle, focusing on achieving them with ease and avoiding burnout. Keep your thoughts clear and concise.
- **Hold the Rosemary/Lavender:** Take the sprig of rosemary or lavender in your hands, close your eyes, and visualize yourself moving through your goals with a sense of calm and ease. Imagine the energy of the moon supporting you, gently pushing you forward without overwhelming you.
- **Affirm Your Intentions:** Hold the paper with your goals in one hand and the sprig of rosemary/lavender in the other. Dip the sprig into the bowl of water and sprinkle a few drops over the paper, saying:

"By water's flow and moon's soft light, I move with ease, my steps are light.
Burnout fades, and joy is near, my goals unfold without fear."

- **Seal the Spell:** Fold the paper and place it under the candle. Let the candle burn for a while, focusing on the flame and the energy of your intentions. When you're ready, extinguish the candle, knowing that the energy of the Waxing Crescent moon will continue to guide you.
- **Create a Reminder:** Keep the folded paper in a place where you'll see it daily, such as on your altar, nightstand, or desk. Each time you see it, take a moment to reconnect with the intention of easeful progress and the energy of the Waxing Crescent moon.

TIME TO GET THINGS DONE

The Waxing Gibbous moon is a time of high energy and productivity, perfect for taking aligned action. This phase is all about getting things done with the full support cf the moon's growing light. Harness this powerful energy to make significant progress on your goals, refine your plans, and push forward with confidence and determination knowing that a week of rest is on its way!

chapter four

THE WAXING GIBBOUS MOON

a 5-7 day phase for aligned action

LET'S GO!!!

As the moon transitions into the Waxing Gibbous phase, I fully embrace this time of heightened energy and focus on getting things done. This phase is all about momentum and action, whereas the ideas and plans from earlier phases are ready to be put into motion. The Waxing Gibbous energy drives us to refine our projects and push forward with determination.

During this phase, I find it crucial to turn my attention to practical tasks and tangible progress. It's the perfect time to tackle the to-do list, make significant strides on projects, and address any challenges that arise. I dive into my work, driven by the knowledge that this is a phase and that I will not have to sustain this level of productivity. Rest is around the corner.

This phase is less about introspection and more about execution. During this phase, I stay productive, keep track of my progress, and adjust my plans as needed. Embracing the Waxing Gibbous energy means I'm actively working towards my goals, making significant headway, and ensuring that every step I take is aligned with my overall vision.

By the end of the Waxing Gibbous phase, I feel accomplished and motivated, having made substantial progress. This period teaches us the value of focused effort and determination, helping build the momentum needed to carry my projects to completion.

Here's what that looked like while I was writing this book:

I use the Waxing Gibbous phase to focus on completing key tasks. After setting my intentions to finalize drafts and prepare for feedback, I channel the moon's energy into action. I tackled each task with purpose, from refining my manuscript to organizing feedback from advanced readers. I made sure to break these tasks into manageable steps and stayed committed to my action plan.

As the Waxing Gibbous phase continued, I found myself leaning into the growing energy with a deep sense of purpose. **This phase, just before the Full Moon, holds a potent mix of anticipation and drive.** It's a time of almost-fullness, where the energy is high but not yet at its peak, allowing for a focused push toward completion.

In this phase, I fully leaned into the opportunity to hyper-focus on my work, ensuring everything was aligned with my original intentions and my ultimate goal. The Waxing Gibbous energy encouraged me to be thorough, pay attention to the details, and ensure the foundation I had laid was solid. This is also the time I tackled action items that felt scary! It's so much easier to complete tasks when you have the force of the moon behind you!

If I ever started to lose momentum or feel overwhelmed, I loved taking time to visualize the finished product, see it in its entirety, and connect with the feelings of accomplishment and fulfillment that would come with its completion. This practice helped to keep me motivated and aligned with the bigger picture, even as I focused on the smaller details. It also helped me enjoy the feelings before the project was even finished!

The process of being in the feelings of the completed goal is the whole point! Everything we do is motivated by feeling a certain way. So if we can tap into those feelings, not only do we feel great along the way (you know your actual life!), but it also calls in more of that same energy making the goal flow toward you with ease! This ,in turn, helps draw more of that energy to you and, in essence, is the basis for manifestation—you being in the feelings allows the Universe to do the rest!

By the end of the Waxing Gibbous phase, I felt a deep sense of readiness. The energy had carried me through a period of intense focus and action, leaving me with an intention that was not only nearly complete but also filled with a sense of purpose and clarity and fulfillment. This phase reminds us that the steps taken before a goal is achieved are just as important as achieving the goal.

WAXING GIBBOUS MOON ENERGY

The Waxing Gibbous moon phase lasts for about a week, bringing a powerful surge of energy and focus. This is the time to take decisive action and push your projects forward with determination. Embrace this phase to make significant progress and bring your goals closer to fruition.

Act

This is a phase of high energy and productivity. With the moon's light almost fully illuminated, you are urged to take aligned action and make significant strides toward your goals. This energy is vibrant and intense, much like the peak energy of summer.

Tip: Look at the action or idea list you made during the Waxing Crescent phase. Choose the action that will give the most momentum and get to work!

Reflect

Reflect on the progress you have made so far and identify areas for improvement. Use this time to review your strategies and make any necessary adjustments. Reflecting now ensures that you are on the right path and ready for the final push toward your goals.

Tip: Regularly assess your progress and make adjustments to your action or to-do list to ensure you're aligning with your main goal and this cycle's focus

Align

This is the time to refine your plans and strategies, ensuring they are in sync with your goals. Channel this energy into focused, purposeful actions that drive progress.

Tip: Stay focused on action steps!

Set Intentions

Set clear and specific intentions to guide your actions during this high-energy phase. Focus on what you need to accomplish to bring your goals closer to fruition.

Tip: These intentions should be actionable and aligned with the progress you want to see.

Perform Rituals

Engage in a ritual that emphasizes productivity and alignment. Review your to-do list and meditate on your vision board to visualize the results ahead so you can stay motivated.

Tip: Create a powerful ritual around a work session so you can see immediate results, fueling your motivation and getting you closer to your goal!

Push Forward

Remember that reaching your goals is a journey, and this phase is about making significant progress. Embrace the momentum and keep pushing forward with determination. Every step you take now brings you closer to achieving your dreams, fueled by the powerful energy of the Waxing Gibbous moon.

ACTION STEPS

With the backing of the moon's growing light, this is the perfect time to make significant strides towards your goals. Focus on executing your plans and pushing forward with determination to turn your intentions into reality, much like the energy of summer.

- **Set Priorities:** Prioritize your tasks and goals based on their importance and urgency. Focus on the most impactful actions that will move you closer to your desired outcomes. This will help you allocate your time and energy effectively during this phase of heightened productivity.

- **Execute Your Plans:** Take concrete steps toward your goals, following through on the plans you've made during previous moon phases. Time to get to it!

- **Seek Support:** Reach out for support or guidance if needed. Whether it's asking for advice from a mentor, delegating tasks to others, or seeking feedback on your plans, don't hesitate to leverage the resources available to you. Collaboration and support can amplify your efforts and accelerate your progress during this phase.

Remember, the energy of doing it all on your own is a lie from capitalistic, patriarchal systems. Community is where it's at!

Moon energy fueling my flow,
I move forward effortlessly
with purpose and passion

How am I maintaining focus and staying committed to my objectives?

In what ways can I fine-tune my plans for greater success?

How am I balancing patience with my desire for progress?

How have my goals and intentions progressed during this phase?

Waxing Gibbous Moon Notes

WAXING GIBBOUS MOON SPELLS & RITUALS

These spells harness the powerful energy of the Waxing Gibbous moon to amplify your productivity and drive. The Waxing Gibbous energy encourages a proactive approach, helping you refine your efforts and tackle tasks with renewed determination.

FOCUS AND DRIVE SPELL

spell purpose: stay focused and determined in accomplishing your goals

when to cast: the Waxing Gibbous   **ritual time:** 15-20 minutes

ingredients:
- yellow or gold candle (for focus and clarity)
- piece of citrine or clear quartz (for energy and clarity)
- small piece of paper and a pen
- sprig of rosemary (for memory and concentration)
- bowl of water

HOW TO PERFORM:

- **Prepare:** Find a quiet space where you won't be disturbed. Set up your materials in front of you, arranging them in a way that feels beautiful.
- **Ground:** Sit comfortably and take a few deep breaths. Visualize roots growing from the base of your spine, anchoring you to the earth. Feel yourself becoming stable and grounded.
- **Light the Candle:** Light the yellow or gold candle. As you do, say these words, "By the light of this candle, I call forth clarity and focus. May its flame ignite my inner drive and illuminate my path."
- **Set Your Intention:** Hold the piece of citrine or clear quartz in your hand. Close your eyes and focus on your intention for enhanced productivity and clarity. Say aloud: "With the energy of the Waxing Gibbous moon, I harness productivity and clear vision. I move forward with determination and purpose."
- **Write Your Goals:** On the piece of paper, write down the key tasks or goals you want to accomplish during this phase. Be specific and concise. Place the piece of paper under the bowl of water. Add the sprig of rosemary to the water. Stir it clockwise three times and say, "As the moon grows, so do my efforts. Rosemary for remembrance; water for flow, clarity, and focus. To my goals I go."
- **Charge the Crystal:** Hold the crystal over the candle flame (not too close) and visualize it absorbing the candle's light and energy. Then, place the crystal in the bowl of water, on top of the paper.
- **Close the Spell:** Sit quietly for a few moments, visualizing yourself completing your tasks with ease and clarity. When you feel ready, say, "With the power of the Waxing Gibbous moon, I am productive and clear. As I say, so shall it be."
- **Complete the Spell:** Extinguish the candle safely. Leave the bowl of water, rosemary, and crystal in a place where they won't be disturbed overnight. In the morning, remove the paper and keep it somewhere you can see it daily. Dispose of the water and rosemary respectfully, and carry the charged crystal with you for continued focus and clarity.

OVERCOMING PROCRASTINATION SPELL

spell purpose: move stuck or stale energy
when to cast: the Waxing Gibbous **ritual time:** 10 minutes
ingredients: yellow candle, pen, and paper

HOW TO PERFORM:

- **Prepare**: Set up a quiet, comfortable space. Light the yellow candle.

- **Focus**: Sit comfortably in front of the candle. Take deep breaths, centering your mind.

- **Set Intentions**: Write down your goals or tasks on the paper. Visualize the completion of these tasks and the sense of accomplishment.

- **Casting the Spell:** Hold the paper close to the flame of the candle (not too close to avoid burning). As it starts to heat up, visualize the energy of the yellow flame infusing into your goals, igniting motivation and focus. Say,
    "With yellow's vibrant glow, procrastination's hold shall go.
    As I focus, my goals will be mine."

- **Close and Express Gratitude:** Take a moment to express gratitude for what you have accomplished so far, acknowledging your efforts and progress. Fold the paper and place it near the candle. Let the candle burn completely or extinguish it while envisioning your productivity, expressing thanks for the motivation and focus you've received.

FOCUSED WORK SESSION

spell purpose: to enhance focus and productivity during a dedicated hour of work

when to cast: the Waxing Gibbous **time:** 10 min + 1 hr session

ingredients: green or white candle (for growth and clarity), paper and pen, and a timer

HOW TO PERFORM:

- **Set the Space:** Arrange your workspace with the candle in front of you. Have the piece of paper and pen ready. Ensure your workspace is free of distractions to maintain focus.

- **Light the Candle**: As you light the candle, say,
  "Under the Waxing Crescent moon's glow, I prepare to focus, let my productivity flow. For the next hour, I channel this light, to work with intent and achieve with might."

- **Write Your Objective:** On the piece of paper, clearly write down the specific task or goal you plan to accomplish during this focused work session. Be precise about what you intend to achieve.

- **Set the Timer:** Set your timer for one hour. This will be your dedicated work period.

- **Complete and Reflect:** When the timer goes off, take a moment to reflect on what you've accomplished. Acknowledge your progress and jot down any notes or observations about what you completed and what's next.

- **Seal the Session:** Extinguish the candle and conclude the spell by expressing gratitude to the moon, the Universe and yourself!

CELEBRATE YOUR JOURNEY AND LET
GO OF WHAT NO LONGER SERVES

The Full Moon phase marks the peak of energy and illumination. Take the time to sit in the light and observe ritual around this fullness each month.

chapter five

THE FULL MOON

a 2-3 day phase to celebrate and release

DANCING UNDER THE MOON

Arguably the most well-know time to hold ritual and gaze at the moon, the Full Moon is where energy peaks and everything is illuminated. It's a powerful time to reflect on the journey that has brought you here, to celebrate your achievements, and to release anything that no longer serves you. This phase invites us to sit in the light of the moon, to observe all that we've created, and to honor the work we've done. It's a moment to acknowledge both the victories and the lessons, as well as to let go of anything that has weighed us down or hindered our progress.

When the Full Moon arrives, it's as if a spotlight is cast on everything we've been working toward. There's no hiding from the truth during this phase; the light of the Full Moon illuminates all aspects of our journey, revealing what has flourished and what needs to be released. This is not just about what we see in the physical realm but also about what is illuminated within us— our emotions, thoughts, and desires.

It's a time of heightened awareness and clarity, where we can clearly see the results of our efforts and make decisions about how to move forward.

As I worked on completing this book, the Full Moon phase became a crucial part of my creative process. Each month, I would take time to sit in the light of the Full Moon and reflect on the progress I had made. This wasn't just a quick review of my to-do list or a check on how many chapters I had written. It was a deeper, more introspective process where I asked myself: What have I accomplished that I'm proud of? What challenges did I face, and how did I overcome them? What do I need to release to continue moving forward with clarity and purpose?

By taking time to work with the Full Moon, I found I was enjoying the process, learning to hear my soul's desires, and finding a more intuitive and fulfilling path to achieving my dreams.

For me, the Full Moon was a time to celebrate even the smallest victories. I would light a candle and hold a ritual of gratitude, thanking myself for the dedication and effort I had put into the book. I celebrated the chapters that flowed effortlessly and the insights that came unexpectedly. But I also took this time to acknowledge the challenges—the moments of doubt, the sections of the book that didn't quite come together as I had hoped, and the times when I felt creatively blocked and wanted to throw the whole thing in the trash!

One Full Moon, I realized I had been holding onto an idea for a chapter that simply wasn't working. It was an idea that I had been attached to from the beginning, but every time I tried to write it, I felt stuck. The Full Moon's light helped me see that this chapter wasn't necessary for the book's overall message. So, I decided to let it go. I performed a simple release ritual, writing down my frustrations and the reasons I was holding onto this idea. Then, under the Full Moon, I burned the paper, symbolically releasing the attachment and the weight it had placed on my creative process. The next day, I felt a sense of lightness and clarity, and the words for the next chapter flowed freely. **Remember: We have the answers we need inside of us already. These rituals and spells just help us pause long enough to hear ourselves.**

The Full Moon phase also served as a reminder to release not just the tangible aspects of the project but also the internal pressures I had placed on myself. I had to let go of the need for perfection, the self-imposed deadlines that didn't align with my natural creative rhythm, and the fear that the book wouldn't be good enough. Each time I released these burdens under the Full Moon, I found that I was able to approach the work with a renewed sense of purpose and joy.

As you reach this phase of your own journey, I encourage you to take full advantage of the Full Moon's energy. Celebrate what you've accomplished, no matter how small or large, and give yourself permission to release what is holding you down and making you feel heavy. The Full Moon is a time of illumination, where everything is brought into the light—your successes, your challenges, your growth. Use this time to honor your journey, to let go of anything weighing you down, and to set yourself up for the next phase with renewed clarity and intention.

FULL MOON ENERGY

The Full Moon phase lasts for about three days. This is the moment to celebrate your progress and reflect on what you've achieved. Embrace this phase to release what no longer serves you and express gratitude for the journey so far.

Connect

As the Full Moon brightens the sky, its energy is vibrant and illuminating. It's a time of culmination, heightened emotions, and realization of intentions set during the new moon.

Tip: For the next three days, take a few minutes to sit under the Full Moon. Allow yourself to savor the beauty as a personal gift while also feeling a deep connection to every other witch who is also gazing at the moon.

Reflect & Celebrate

Harness the Full Moon's energy by reflecting on the intentions you set during the New Moon. What progress have you made? Celebrate your achievements and acknowledge how far you've come.

Tip: Block out time on your calendar for the next four to six Full Moons so you can fully immerse yourself in your rituals.

Align

This is an opportunity to realign your energies with the intentions you set. Embrace the Full Moon's energy to affirm your desires, ensuring they are still in harmony with your heart's truest aspirations.

Tip: Use the Full Moon's light to check in with your intentions and ensure that they still resonate with your heart's deepest desires.

Acknowledge

Just like an artist steps back to evaluate their progress and adjust their brushstrokes, it's time to assess the work you've done and appreciate the steps you've taken. Reflect on what you've achieved so far and celebrate the positive changes that are emerging.

Tip: Reflect on what you've manifested and take time to acknowledge and celebrate the positive changes and successes you've reaped.

Release

As the moon wanes, it's a moment to release what no longer serves you. Reflect on any obstacles or patterns hindering your progress. Let go of negativity or self-doubt, making space for new growth.

Tip: Journal about any obstacles or doubts, then symbolically release them—such as by tearing up the paper—to clear space for new growth.

Perform Rituals

This is a time to celebrate your achievements and let go of the heavy. Engage in a ritual that resonates with you, whether it's a simple meditation or a more elaborate ceremony. Embrace this moment to realign with your goals and intentions.

Embrace

The Full Moon isn't just an endpoint; it's a part of your ongoing journey. Embrace the process, remain open to opportunities, and continue to evolve as you move through the cycles of life.

UNCOVERING SHOULDS:
A PRE-RITUAL REFLECTION

This might just be the most
powerful magic I have to offer you.
Please come back to this as often as you need.

Did you complete everything you hoped for in the Waxing Gibbous phase? Do you feel behind, like you should have done more? These feelings are common because we've been conditioned from birth to have unrealistic expectations of ourselves.

The word "should" subtly controls our lives, dictating how we think and act. From a young age, we've been taught by our caregivers, religions, and society that certain beliefs and expectations are truths we must follow.

These "shoulds" are heavy burdens we carry, often without even realizing it. **But here's the truth: many of these expectations don't belong to us; they were handed to us, and we've mistaken them as our own**. Releasing these burdens is one of the greatest gifts we can give ourselves!

When you catch yourself saying, "I should have...," recognize it as a powerful opportunity to lighten your load. Follow the steps to identify where this "should" thought came from, and then use the Unbinding Spell on page 93 to free yourself from these expectations. By doing so, you reclaim your energy and align more closely with your true self.

Each one of these steps is VERY important. Make sure you complete all four. Don't skip a step!

1. Ask yourself, "What do I think I should be doing?" or "What is the 'should' thought that I had?" You can't change the thought if you don't know what it is!
*Example: I am lazy if I rest. If my partner is around, I **should** be up cleaning so they don't think I'm wasting time.*

2. Ask yourself, "Where did this thought come from?" Usually it was given to us by our parents, religion, or society when we were five to ten years old. Once you realize the thought is based in patriarchy, capitalism, or sexism and not your actual truth, this will often give you the motivation you need to break the thought pattern!
Example: I always saw my mom hop up when my dad got home. She was always working when he was around. This thought is based in the belief that as a woman I should serve. My dad never rested because he said it was lazy and a waste of time.

3. Ask yourself, "Is this true?"
Example: No, rest is neccesary and a human right. I don't have to earn rest. Lazy is a made-up concept based in capitalism and meant to exhaust me.

4. Ask yourself, "What is my new truth?" **PLEASE NOTE:** It is very important to give yourself something to say to replace this old thought. Give yourself grace. This old thought has had many, many years to wear a path in your brain. Gently correct yourself each time you tell yourself the old lie. Over time, your truth will become the new habit!
Example: Rest is a human right. Rest is not earned!

1. _____
_____
2. _____
_____
3. _____
_____
4. _____
_____

ACTION STEPS

Much like the zenith of summer before the transition into autumn, this two to three day period is perfect for acknowledging your progress, letting go of what no longer serves you, and celebrating your achievements. Use this powerful time to reflect, release, and rejoice.

- **Reflect and Release:** Take time to reflect on your journey and identify any thoughts, habits, or obstacles that are holding you back. Write them down on a piece of paper and, in a symbolic gesture, burn the paper (safely) to release these burdens and create space for new opportunities.
- **Celebrate Your Successes:** Acknowledge and celebrate the progress you have made and the goals you have achieved. Treat yourself to something special, gather with loved ones, or engage in a joyful activity that honors your efforts and accomplishments.
- **Practice Gratitude:** Make a list of things you are grateful for, focusing on the positive aspects of your journey and the support you have received. Share your gratitude with others or perform a gratitude ritual to amplify the positive energy in your life.
- **Connect with the Moon:** Spend some time outside under the Full Moonlight. Meditate or simply sit quietly, allowing the moon's energy to wash over you and recharge your spirit. Focus on feeling connected to the larger universe and the natural cycles of life, drawing strength and clarity from the moon's illumination.

Under the glow of the
Full Moon,
I release what no longer serves me

What aspects of my life feel illuminated and brought to completion?

What accomplishments or manifestations am I celebrating at this peak?

How can I express gratitude for the abundance present in my life?

How have my emotions been heightened during this phase?

Full Moon Notes

FULL MOON
SPELLS & RITUALS

These spells are designed to help build confidence, create momentum, and foster the conditions needed for growth and progress. The Waxing Crescent energy supports the gentle unfolding of your intentions, helping to bring them into reality without overwhelming you.

FULL MOON RITUAL

purpose: releasing what no longer serves, celebrating growth

when to hold: on the Full Moon

ritual time: 30-45 minutes

ingredients:
- white or silver candles to symbolize the moon's brightness and purity
- incense or smudge stick for cleansing and clearing the space
- journal and pen to write down reflections, accomplishments, and what you want to release
- one or more crystals that resonate with the energy of the Full Moon (such as clear quartz, moonstone, or selenite)
- optional items: incense, essential oils, altar decorations, or any other items that hold personal significance or symbolic value

HOW TO PERFORM:

Prepare: Find a quiet and comfortable space where you won't be disturbed. Clear the area with incense or use a smudge stick to cleanse the energy.

Center Yourself: Light your candle(s) and any incense or diffuse essential oils, if desired. Create a serene ambiance. Take a few deep breaths to ground yourself. Close your eyes and set your intention for the ritual, focusing on what you wish to release or celebrate.

Reflect and Write: Reflect on your achievements since the last Full Moon. Take your journal or paper and write down what you're proud of and what you're ready to release. Express gratitude for what has come to fruition.

Release: Use a separate piece of paper to write down what you're releasing. Visualize these things leaving your life. Burn this paper safely in the flame of the candle, allowing the energy to be released to the Universe.

Celebrate: Hold your crystal(s) in your hands, infusing them with your intentions. Meditate or simply take a moment to bask in the moon's energy, feeling gratitude for your accomplishments.

Close: Express gratitude for the experience. Blow out the candle(s) or let them burn out naturally if safety allows.

Notes:

AN UNBINDING SPELL

spell purpose: let go of old beliefs   **ritual time:** 10 minutes

when to cast: any time, most potent on Full Moon

ingredients: white candle (for purification and clarity), black candle (for banishing and releasing), herbs associated with release and transformation (such as sage, rosemary, or cedar), fire-safe bowl or cauldron, piece of paper and pen

HOW TO PERFORM:

- **Preparation**: Set up your materials in a safe, fireproof space. Take a few deep breaths to ground yourself.
- **Written Release:** Take the piece of paper and write down the old belief you want to release. Pour your emotions and intentions into this writing.
- **Empowerment**: Hold the paper in your hands and visualize the old belief losing its hold on you. Read aloud what you've written, affirming your decision to let it go.
- **Herbal Infusion**: Prepare a small bowl or container with the chosen herbs. Hold it and visualize these herbs absorbing the energy of release and transformation.
- **Candle Ritual:** Light the white candle, symbolizing purification and clarity. As it burns, visualize it cleansing your space and mind from the remnants of the old belief. Light the black candle, representing banishment and release. Feel its energy aiding you in letting go of the old belief.
- **Burning Ceremony:** Safely ignite the paper with the black candle's flame. As it burns, visualize the old belief turning into ash, dissipating into the air, and becoming no longer part of your reality.
- **Herbal Blessing:** Sprinkle a small amount of herbs onto the burning paper, infusing it with the energy of release and transformation.
- **Closing**: Express gratitude to the elements, the candles, and the herbs for their assistance. Feel a sense of lightness and freedom as you let go of the old belief.
- **Return:** Allow ashes to cool before disposing of them outside, returning them to the earth as a symbol of the completed release.

Remember, the true magic lies within your belief and intention. Focus on your newfound truth and let the spell strengthen your commitment to living authentically.

FULL MOON REJUVENATION SPELL

spell purpose: let go of old beliefs

when to cast: on the Full Moon or within a day before or after, when the moon's energy is still potent

ritual time: 30-60 minutes

ingredients:
- Epsom salt or sea salt
- essential oils: lavender, sandalwood, rose, or chamomile (for their calming and cleansing properties)
- herbs: dried rosemary, chamomile flowers, or calendula petals (for their soothing and purifying effects)
- crystals: clear quartz, moonstone, amethyst, or selenite (to amplify lunar energies and intention setting)

HOW TO PERFORM:

- **Cleanse the Bath Water:** Fill your bathtub with warm water. Add Epsom salts, a few drops of essential oil, and herbs to the water. Stir clockwise, infusing the water with your intentions for release and renewal. You might also charge the water by placing crystals around the tub or directly in the water.
- **Enter the Sacred Space:** Before entering the bath, stand near it or sit beside it. Close your eyes, take deep breaths, and visualize yourself surrounded by white or purifying light. Set your intentions for the ritual: what you wish to release and what you want to manifest.
- **Immerse in the Ritual Bath:** Slowly step into the bath, feeling the water enveloping you. Visualize the water cleansing away any negativity or old energies. As you soak, focus on your intentions, repeating affirmations or prayers that resonate with your goals. Feel the moon's energy washing over you, purifying your body, mind, and spirit.
- **Soak In:** Relax in the bath, letting go of tension and allowing the energies of the Full Moon to recharge you. Meditate, visualize your desires, or simply be present in the moment, feeling the transformative energy of the water and the moon.
- **Close with Gratitude:** When you feel ready to conclude the ritual, slowly rise from the bath. Visualize the water carrying away all that no longer serves you as it drains. Feel renewed, light, and aligned with your intentions.
- **Ground and Integrate:** After the bath, take a moment to ground yourself. You might sit quietly, journal your experiences. Express gratitude to the moon, the elements, and any deities or energies you invoked during the ritual.

Remember, the key to any ritual is your intention and focus. Allow yourself to be present in the moment and open to the energies surrounding you during this Full Moon bath ritual.

TIME TO WRAP IT UP

As the moon starts to wane, the next phase is all about closing up projects and pausing tasks so you can easily move into a week of rest. What needs to be completed so your mind can rest easy? What needs to be released?

chapter six

THE WANING
GIBBOUS MOON

a 5-7 day phase for sacred release

WINDING DOWN

As the moon begins its descent into the Waning Gibbous phase, it ushers in a period of winding down and preparation for rest. This phase is all about completing projects, pausing tasks, and ensuring that you're ready to fully enjoy a well-deserved break. Think of this time as preparing for a vacation. Just like you would finalize details and clear your to-do list before stepping away, use the Waning Gibbous moon to wrap up your current responsibilities and release any lingering stress.

For me, working on this book during the Waning Gibbous moon was an exciting part of the process. I used this time to focus on closing out tasks and ensuring that everything was in order before taking a break. I made a detailed list of what needed to be completed—final edits, sending out manuscript drafts, and addressing any last-minute revisions. Each work session, I made my way through this checklist, tackling the most pressing items first while being mindful not to rush. **I knew that the goal was to finish enough to allow for a restful break, not to push myself to complete everything in a frantic hurry.**

During this phase, I also took time to pause and consider what I could release. I reflected on aspects of the project that were either causing stress or no longer aligned with my vision. This included letting go of perfectionist tendencies and unrealistic deadlines that had been weighing on me. I allowed myself to acknowledge and release these pressures, making space for a more relaxed and productive period of rest.

To prepare practically, I prioritized completing key aspects of the book and paused any additional work that could wait until after my break. This helped to ensure a smooth transition and allowed me to step away with confidence that my work was in good shape.

Remember, the Waning Gibbous moon is not a time to rush or push through your remaining tasks. Instead, it's about gently completing what you can and pausing what needs more time. By addressing your responsibilities without added pressure, you create a clear and calm space for yourself. This approach ensures that when you do take your break, you can fully enjoy it without the weight of unfinished business or lingering stress. If you've ever tried to take a break with unfinished tasks hanging over your head, you know why this phase is so important! Because if you are not able to rest, then when that energy starts to build with the next Waxing Crescent and Waxing Gibbous, you won't have the energy you need to work on your goal.

As I mentioned earlier, move through this phase the same way you'd prepare for a vacation—organize, finalize, and release, so you can fully embrace the coming rest period. Just as careful planning and preparation make a vacation more enjoyable, your efforts during the Waning Gibbous moon will set the stage for a more refreshing and restorative break. By completing what you can and letting go of what no longer serves you, you create the conditions for a peaceful and rejuvenating rest.

As the Waning Gibbous moon draws to a close, the day before the Waxing Crescent phase presents a perfect opportunity to pause and reflect on your journey. In a world that sometimes feels like a bullet train, this is the perfect moment to consider how far you've come and what you've achieved, as well as to contemplate the next steps in your ongoing process of growth and renewal. Use the questions from the following page to help you with this reflection.

THIRD QUARTER REFLECTION

Reflecting on Achievements: What significant accomplishments or progress have you made since the beginning of the cycle? Write about the things you're proud of and how they align with your long-term aspirations.

Fine-Tuning Patterns: What aspects of your goals or routines need fine-tuning or adjustment? Are there any patterns or habits that hindered your progress during this phase?

Letting Go: What thoughts, habits, or goals no longer serve your growth? Reflect on what you're ready to release to create space for new intentions.

Identifying Priorities: Considering your broader goals, what specific areas or tasks need your attention in the next phase? List them in order of importance and relevance to your long-term vision.

Incorporating Restorative Practices: What self-care or rejuvenating practices can you incorporate to replenish your energy during this resting phase? How will these practices support your overall well-being?

Setting Intentions for the Future: What are your intentions for the next moon cycle? Frame your goals using positive and affirming language, focusing on what you want to invite into your life.

Embracing Patience: How can you practice patience and trust in the process during this resting phase? Reflect on the importance of allowing things to unfold in their own time.

WANING GIBBOUS ENERGY

The Waning Gibbous moon phase lasts five to seven days, providing a reflective window for completing projects and preparing for rest. This period is ideal for tying up loose ends. Use this time to evaluate your goal and New Moon intention and create space for the rest that follows.

Let Go

The Waning Gibbous phase embodies a period of release, reflection, and closure. It signifies a time for letting go and making space for rest.

Tip: Embrace the Waning Gibbous phase by taking time to journal about any limiting beliefs and reflect on the progress you've made.

Reflect

This is a time to pause, assess progress, and contemplate the lessons learned along the way. Through journaling, we can deepen our understanding of ourselves and our path, identifying any unhelpful habits we don't want to carry forward and deciding the direction we want to take in the next lunar cycle.

Align

This phase invites us to reflect on lessons learned, declutter our minds, and cleanse our spirits. In the gentle glow of the waning moon, we find solace in surrendering to the natural ebb and flow of life.

Tip: Dance to help release stagnant energy from your body, letting the waning moon's energy guide your release and renewal.

Set Intentions

By consciously releasing old patterns, negative beliefs, and stagnant energy, we pave the way for growth, healing, and transformation. Setting intentions aligned with this energy allows us to trust that what is released will make room for what is meant to enter our lives next.

Tip: Take a few moments to write down what you wish to release, then perform a symbolic act of letting go, such as burning the paper or burying it in the earth. Trust that this act of release will create space for new opportunities and growth.

Complete

This is an ideal time to wrap up projects, tie up loose ends, and let go of anything that no longer serves our highest good. Engaging in rituals such as journaling to reflect on lessons learned, decluttering physical and mental spaces, and practicing forgiveness and gratitude can be particularly potent during this phase.

Tip: Use this time to complete tasks and clear mental clutter, setting the stage for a restorative break.

Embrace

Waning Gibbous energy calls us to acknowledge the progress we have made and the challenges we have overcome. Just as the moon sheds its light, you're encouraged to release what holds you back, trusting that every step you take brings you closer to your true power.

Tip: A witch is incredibly powerful when she fully accepts both the light and darkness within. You are beautiful as is. Allow yourself to gleefully throw away any thoughts that do not support that!

THE WEIGHT OF EMOTIONS

Emotions are the rhythms of our inner landscape, yet when these rhythms get disrupted or stuck, they create a resistance in our bodies that can affect us profoundly. In their book *Burnout*, Emily and Amelia Nagoski explore the physical effects of emotional congestion, showing us how unprocessed feelings can weigh heavily on us.

Emotional Stagnation and Its Impact

When emotions get trapped or remain unexpressed, they don't simply vanish. Instead, they find refuge in our bodies, showing up as tension, exhaustion, or physical discomfort. ***This accumulation of emotional stress can lead to a state of chronic stress response, impacting our nervous system and overall well-being.***

The stress response cycle is incomplete if emotions aren't processed entirely. These unresolved emotions linger, resulting in a continuous state of stress that affects both our mental and physical health.

The Importance of Release

Acknowledging and releasing these emotions becomes crucial for our emotional and physical health. Through practices like movement, dance, and other forms of physical expression, we create an outlet for these stagnant emotions, allowing them to flow and dissipate.

By engaging in rituals that promote emotional release, we honor our feelings and grant ourselves permission to let go. These practices are not merely about purging emotions but also reclaiming our bodies, restoring balance, and fostering a sense of ease and freedom.

Moving Toward Liberation

Embracing the practices of movement, dance, or other physical excersice can be a transformative step in releasing pent-up emotions. As we engage in these rituals, we invite the trapped emotions to surface, allowing them to flow out and free us from their weight.

THE POWER OF JUMPING AND SHAKING

When we are pursuing life-changing goals (or let's be honest, just living our lives as women), we experience stress and our bodies enter a state of heightened alertness. This response prepares us either to confront or escape from perceived threats. However, in modern life, many of our stressors are not physical threats we can fight or flee from, leaving our bodies stuck in this state of readiness without a clear way to release the tension.

My go-to way to release these emotions and complete the stress cycle is through jumping or shaking. This technique not only helps to discharge accumulated stress but also leaves you feeling refreshed and rejuvenated. As a bonus, it's super simple and always available.

Physical exertion, such as jumping or shaking, mimics the physical activity our bodies are prepared for during the fight-or-flight response. This movement helps to "complete" the stress cycle by providing an outlet for the built-up energy, allowing our bodies to return to a state of calm.

The Benefits of Jumping and Shaking

1. **Releasing Pent-Up Emotions:** These movements allow you to physically express and release emotions like frustration, overwhelm, and anger by dislodging these emotions from where they might be stored in your body.
2. **Reducing Physical Tension**: Stress often manifests as muscle tension, particularly in areas like the shoulders, neck, and back. By jumping or shaking, you can help to loosen these tight muscles, reducing physical discomfort.
3. **Boosting Endorphins:** Physical activity stimulates the release of endorphins, the body's natural feel-good hormones. These endorphins can help to improve your mood, counteracting feelings of anger or frustration.

Begin by gently bouncing on your toes or lightly shaking your hands and arms. Gradually increase the intensity of your movements, focusing on the areas where you feel the most tension.

When you feel like you can't jump and shake anymore, allow your body to slowly come to a rest. Take deep breaths and notice the shift in your energy. Next time you feel overwhelmed by stress, take a deep breath and literally shake it off!

EASE AND FLOW

Below are other powerful ways to release stagnant emotions from the body. Find what works for you and do your best to add this movement to each day - giving you a way to step out of the system that the patriarchy put in place to keep us quiet, stuck, and small.

Ecstatic Dance

This practice is simply allowing your body to move in whatever way it wants while music is playing. Allow the music to guide your body, shedding inhibitions and inviting raw emotion to surface. (I lock my door so I can relax and not worry about someone seeing me!) Move freely, intuitively, and without judgment. With each jump, shake, or flow, you are liberating emotions stored within muscles, joints, and the very fibers of your being.

This free-flowing movement permits emotions to emerge, unravel, and dissipate, freeing trauma patterns and regulating the nervous system. Allow yourself to **move as a *feeling*** without restraint for five to twenty minutes. The keys to this movement are keeping the eyes closed and moving continuously.

Breathwork

Breathwork involves practicing intentional breathing techniques designed to promote relaxation, reduce stress, and improve emotional well-being. By focusing on your breath, you can bring your attention to the present moment, calming the mind and body. This type of breathing helps to dislodge trapped emotions and invites a sense of spaciousness and calmness into your being.

Do Something

There are many ways to complete the stress cycle and release tension. What DOESN'T work is just telling yourself everything will be ok. Weightlifting, running, swimming, laughing, sharing affection, crying, creatively expressing yourself, progressively tensing one muscle after the other while imagining vividly beating the daylights out of the stressor... They all have one thing in common—doing something. See additional reading and resources on page 156 to dive deeper.

ACTION STEPS

During the Waning Gibbous moon phase, we honor the energy of release and completion. This is a time to wrap up projects, tie up loose ends, and let go of anything that no longer serves our highest good.

- **Practice the Restful Wrap-Up Spell:** Use this to make a list of what you want to complete so that your mind will have the space to relax during the upcoming Waning Crescent moon. Remember, you can simply bring something to a pause knowing you can return when the resting energy shifts.

- **Complete Unfinished Tasks:** Take your list and prioritize what needs to be completed before the end of the lunar cycle. This is not the time for a push or to add more to your plate. It's a time to wrap up anything pressing so you can truly rest.

- **Declutter Your Space:** The Waning Gibbous is a great time to clear out physical clutter from your living or working environment. Donate or discard items that no longer serve a purpose, creating space for new energy to flow.

- **Move Trapped Emotions:** Is there a heaviness in your body or mind? This could be emotions trapped and waiting for release. Use this time to move them out! How can you incorporate movement into your everyday?

I let my emotions flow,
transform, & set me free

What do I need to complete to transition out of this phase with clarity and be ready for rest?

What lessons or insights am I learning from recent experiences?

What self-care practices support me during this period of closure?

What intentions or goals am I preparing to release or adjust?

Waning Gibbous Moon Notes

WANING GIBBOUS MOON SPELLS & RITUALS

These spells are designed to help with releasing lingering, stuck emotions and wrapping up any remaining loose ends in your projects. This phase supports the completion of tasks and emotional release, helping you to prepare for a period of rest and renewal.

COLORFUL FLOW SPELL

spell purpose: channel emotions through color

when to cast: any time   **ritual time:** 15-20 minutes

ingredients: canvas or sketchbook, paints, paintbrush

HOW TO PERFORM:

- **Set the Space:** Find a quiet, comfortable area where you can be undisturbed.
- **Center:** Take a few moments to ground yourself. Close your eyes, breathe deeply, and connect with your emotions. Use the feelings wheel (see Chapter 10) to name your emotions. Say your feeling out loud and allow it to be ok.
- **Conduct Emotion:** Pick up your painting tools. Envision them as conduits for your emotions, extensions of your feelings.
- **Infuse Emotion:** Begin without a predetermined image in mind. Allow your emotions to guide the colors that emerge.
- **Allow to Flow:** Dip your brush into the colors that resonate with your emotions. Let your hand move freely, allowing the colors to express your feelings on the canvas or paper.
- **Release:** Imagine your emotions flowing through your arm, into the colors, and onto the page. Release any judgment or expectations.
- **Reflect:** Take breaks to reflect on the emotions being channeled. Observe the patterns, hues, and intensity of colors used, recognizing them as representations of your inner world. Has your feeling shifted and morphed into another feeling?
- **Close:** When your emotions have been expressed, conclude the session. Acknowledge and express gratitude for the emotional release and the creative journey undertaken.

Note: This practice isn't about creating a specific image but about allowing your feelings to freely flow through the colors onto the canvas or paper, creating a visual representation of your emotional landscape.

RESTFUL WRAP-UP SPELL

spell purpose: energetically close each open task so you can allow yourself to rest in the next phase

when to cast: the **Waning Crescent ritual time:** 15-20 min.

ingredients: white candle, paper and pen, lavender essential oil or dried lavender, bowl of water

HOW TO PERFORM:

- **Center Yourself:** Take a few deep breaths, grounding yourself in the present moment. Light the white candle, representing purity and clarity.
- **Take Inventory:** Take the piece of paper and pen. Write down each task or project that you need to wrap up or complete before your rest period. Be specific and concise. Once you've listed all your tasks, fold the paper and hold it between your palms. Close your eyes and visualize each task being completed successfully. Feel a sense of relief and satisfaction wash over you as you imagine each project coming to a close.
- **Release:** Place a drop of lavender essential oil on the folded paper or sprinkle some dried lavender over it. Lavender is associated with relaxation and tranquility, enhancing the spell's energy of rest. Dip your fingertips into the bowl of water and sprinkle a few drops over the candle flame. As you do this, visualize any remaining stress or tension dissipating, leaving only a sense of peace and calm.
- **Energetically Seal:** Hold the paper over the candle flame (but be cautious not to burn it). As it heats up, imagine the energy of the flame sealing each task with finality, allowing you to let go and move forward. Once you feel that each task has been energetically sealed, extinguish the candle.
- **Close with Gratitude:** Keep the folded paper in a safe place until you've completed all the tasks listed on it. Once you've finished everything, you can dispose of the paper by burning it (safely) or burying it in the earth as a symbol of closure. Take a moment to express gratitude for the completion of your tasks and the opportunity to rest and recharge.

Note: Magic is a tool to enhance intention and focus. It's important to take practical steps in the physical world to complete your tasks and prepare for rest. Use this spell as a complement to your actions and intentions.

DANCE OF LIBERATION SPELL

spell purpose: emotional release and energy alignment

when to cast: any time   **ritual time:** 15-20 minutes

ingredients: A private space for movement—preferably with a locking door, your favorite playlist without words, smudge stick or incense (optional)

HOW TO PERFORM:

- **Prepare**: Create a clear, open space for movement. Cleanse the space with incense if desired.
- **Create a Playlist:** Curate a playlist that transitions through various emotional tones, from upbeat and energizing to angry, sad, and contemplative.
- **Move:** Play the music and let yourself move freely, allowing yourself to release any stuck or pent-up emotions. This is a time to get out of your head and allow your body to move as a feeling. Feeling angry? Move like anger!
- **Embrace the Flow:** As you move, visualize emotions leaving your body with each step and dance motion. Feel the weight lifting off your shoulders as you express and release these emotions through movement.
- **Close**: Once the playlist ends, stand still and take deep breaths. Feel the space you've created within yourself. Thank the energies around you and embrace the sense of liberation.

Note: Not able to dance? You can do this in a chair, hands and knees, or while lying down... simply move what you can. You can even find release by imagining dancing or moving and the feelings flowing out of your body!

REST

As the moon wanes to complete darkness, this phase is a chance to give your mind and body time to release the pressures of productivity and perfectionism, allowing you to exhale and slip into deep, guilt-free rest. Trust that surrendering to this rest will allow you to emerge renewed and ready to embrace the next phase of your journey.

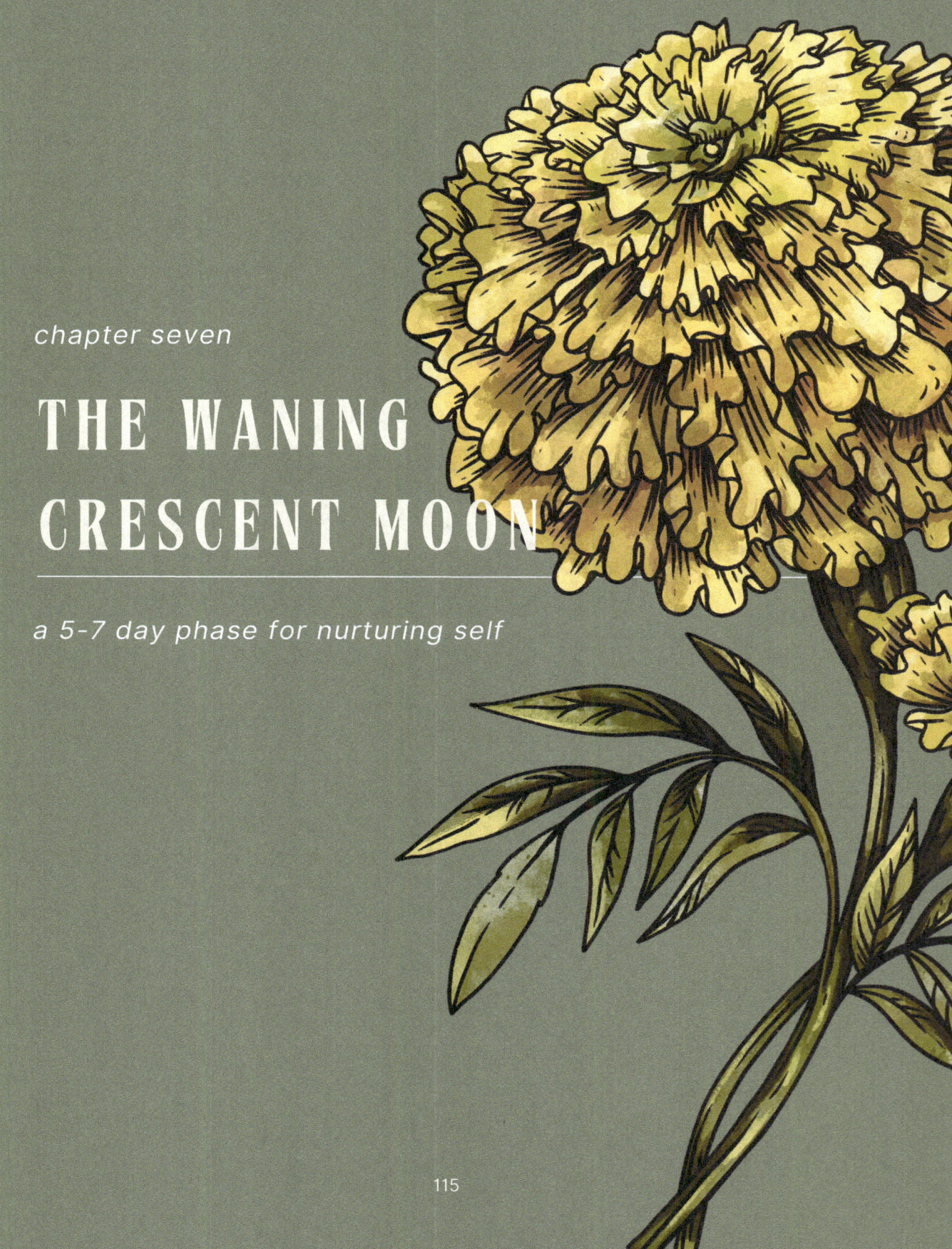

chapter seven

THE WANING CRESCENT MOON

a 5-7 day phase for nurturing self

PREPARING FOR NEW BEGINNINGS

As the moon transitions into the Waning Crescent phase, it signals a gentle winding down. This phase, though often overshadowed by the more dynamic stages of the lunar cycle, holds a profound secret for witches: it is the optimal period for rest and reflection. Embracing this phase allows you to recharge, clear your mind, and prepare yourself energetically for the next cycle of growth and action.

I tend to go full steam ahead and rush to complete a project. This, of course, is the perfect breeding ground for burnout, and—even sadder—a loss of passion for my desires and dreams. For me, while writing this book, the Waning Crescent phase became an essential part of my creative process. When I let my pursuit of goals follow the moon, I allowed myself this time to step back and reflect on the journey so far. This period of rest was not just a break but also a vital component of the creative cycle that allowed me to gather my strength and insights.

During the Waning Crescent, I made a conscious effort to slow down and take care of myself. **Instead of pushing through exhaustion or forcing productivity, I embraced the natural rhythm of the moon and allowed myself to rest.** This included setting aside specific times for relaxation, spending more time alone in nature, and engaging in activities that replenished my energy. I made sure there was less on the calendar with others so I could have more time for cocooning.

By integrating periods of rest and reflection into our routine, we honor the cyclical nature of our energy and avoid the pitfalls of burnout. **This phase teaches us that rest is not a luxury but rather a necessary part of our creative and personal growth.**

Taking time to rest during the Waning Crescent phase ensures that we enter the new cycle with a full reserve of energy and enthusiasm. **When we allow ourselves to step back and rejuvenate, we return to our goals and projects with a clearer mind and a more vibrant spirit.** This intentional pause makes it easier to dive into the next phase with renewed focus and creativity, setting the stage for a productive and fulfilling new beginning.

By respecting the Waning Crescent as a time for self-care and reflection, you prepare yourself to engage fully in the new cycle ahead, ensuring that each phase of your journey is met with the energy and clarity you need to succeed.

WANING CRESECENT ENERGY

The Waning Crescent phase lasts for five to seven days, providing a quiet and nurturing window for cocooning and rest. This is ideal for allowing yourself time to recharge before the New Moon. Embrace this period to rest deeply, letting go of guilt and preparing to emerge renewed for the next cycle of growth.

Embrace

Embracing this period as an opportunity for restorative rest enables you to replenish your energy reserves and prepare for the new beginnings that await you in the upcoming lunar cycle.

Tip: Make note of any guilt that surfaces when you try to rest. Take time to journal or cast a guilt release spell so you can sink into rest.

Reflect

This phase offers a sacred space for quiet contemplation, allowing you to sift through thoughts, emotions, and insights with clarity and honesty. It also empowers you to make meaning out of your journey, honor your growth, and prepare for the new beginnings that lie ahead in the next lunar cycle.

Tip: Mark this phase on your calendar so you can avoid scheduling too many activities that keep you from slowing down.

Align

Trust in the natural process of closure and completion. Allow yourself to loosen your hold on everything and find clarity in stillness. Find quietness and listen to your intuition.

Set Intentions

Setting intentions centered around resting involves prioritizing self-care, rejuvenation, and inner reflection. It's a time to honor the body's need for deep rest and recuperation, allowing ourselves to unwind from the demands of daily life without guilt or pressure.

Tip: This is the time to be selfish. Saying no (even to good things) is ok!

Create

Create sacred spaces of retreat where you can withdraw from the external world and turn inward. Practices such as meditation, gentle movement, or simply sitting in silence are ways to provide a sanctuary for rest and rejuvenation, allowing you to emerge refreshed and ready to embrace the next phase.

Tip: Channel your inner cat and create a cozy nook to hide away in. Stock it with your favorite books, crystals, oracle decks, and other witch tools.

Be Patient

As you learn to release the pressure to constantly strive and achieve, remember to be gentle with yourself. Unlearning the deeply ingrained demands of capitalism and patriarchy is a gradual process, one that requires patience and self-compassion. One cycle at a time, you will move closer to the guilt-free rest that is your birthright.

Tip: If you feel like you aren't "doing it right" and tend to speak harshly to yourself, think about how you would talk to little you. Imagine yourself at 7 or 8 and practice speaking gently and lovingly.

REST IS REVOLUTION

Embracing the Power of Rest

Rest is a radical act, a revolutionary notion to us now but one that has been built into the fabric of our bodies and the world since the beginning of time! Just like spring growth and transformation arise only AFTER a time of winter rest, we too need rest to be productive. Rest is not just idleness; it's a profound act of self-care and resistance against a culture that praises perpetual productivity. **Rest invites us to honor the sanctity of our being and acknowledge that growth and evolution emerge from the spaces of pause.** In these moments of stillness, ideas germinate, creativity flourishes, and true healing begins.

Tricia Hersey, known for her pioneering work with the Nap Ministry, advocates for the liberation found in rest. She emphasizes how rest challenges societal constructs, especially for marginalized communities historically denied the luxury of rest. This revolution of rest is a reclaiming of our time and well-being.

Remembering Ancient Wisdom

Deeply connected with nature and its cycles, witches have always known the power of rest. However, because this wisdom led to confident, powerful women, it was feared, demonized, and taken away from us. Now, we often believe the lie that our productivity will make us happier, our exhaustion will show our worth, and our hard work will gain us admiration. But when we take two steps back and see who benefits from us believing those thoughts, we can start to deconstruct the lies we have taken on and learn from the women before us. By embracing rest as a form of resistance and healing, we confront societal expectations and cultivate a nurturing relationship with ourselves.

When we follow the seasons, the moon, and our own body's cycles, we reclaim our sacred power. The more we allow deep rest, the more powerful we become. Deep healing rest, time alone, and not-doing lead to restoration and a renewal of energy to propel us into the work of the next cycle.

119

EMBRACING REST

In a world urging constant productivity, it's crucial to redefine what rest truly embodies. It's the gentle art of saying no to what drains your energy and yes to what rejuvenates your spirit. Here are eight ways to incorporate rest into your life.

Active Rest: Laying in bed all day can actually make you more tired! Engage in light movement or stretching exercises to release physical tension.

Pleasurable Eating: Relish a meal with undivided attention, savoring each bite mindfully.

Digital Detox: Screens are known to drain our energy and make us tired. Disconnect from screens for a few hours or a day to offer your mind respite.

Artistic Expression: Unleash creativity through painting, sculpting, crocheting, or your favorite creative outlet.

Musical Connection: Immerse yourself in songs that uplift or calm you.

Emotional Release: Through journaling or sharing thoughts with a trusted friend, give your brain a break and unburden your emotional load.

Plant Care: The act of watering, pruning, or simply observing plants fosters a sense of calm, grounding you in the present moment and promoting relaxation.

Sacred Spaces: Tidying altars, cleaning tools, working with crystals and herbs, and decluttering magical spaces offers a sense of clarity and peace.

SELF-CARE CHECKLIST

These activities are aimed at providing opportunities for deep rest, introspection, and rejuvenation as you align with the rest that the Waning Crescent energy calls for.

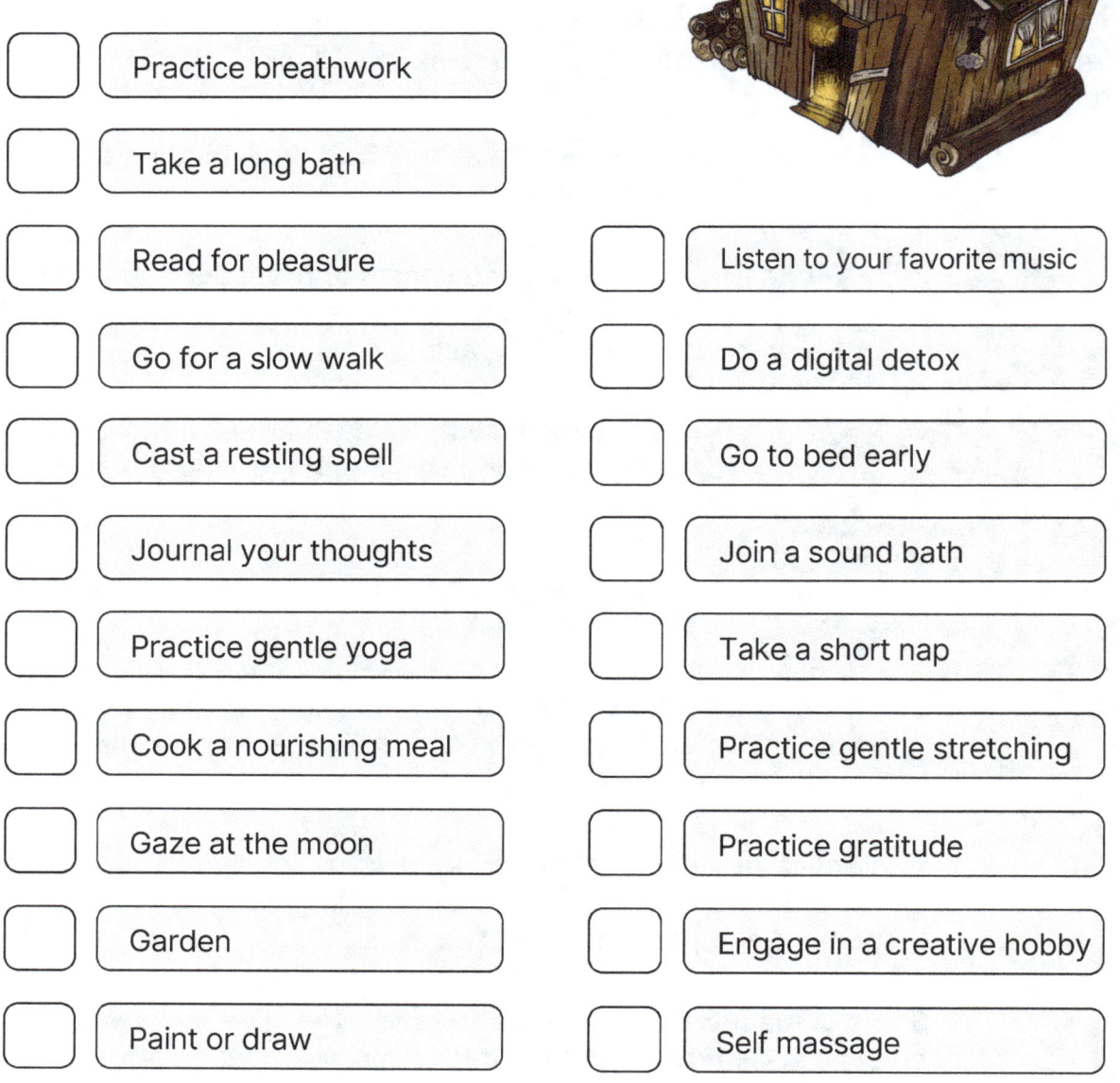

- [ ] Practice breathwork
- [ ] Take a long bath
- [ ] Read for pleasure
- [ ] Go for a slow walk
- [ ] Cast a resting spell
- [ ] Journal your thoughts
- [ ] Practice gentle yoga
- [ ] Cook a nourishing meal
- [ ] Gaze at the moon
- [ ] Garden
- [ ] Paint or draw

- [ ] Listen to your favorite music
- [ ] Do a digital detox
- [ ] Go to bed early
- [ ] Join a sound bath
- [ ] Take a short nap
- [ ] Practice gentle stretching
- [ ] Practice gratitude
- [ ] Engage in a creative hobby
- [ ] Self massage

ACTION STEPS

It's time to honor the call for rest and relaxation. Find pockets of time and space to allow yourself sacred rejuvenation.

- While it would be amazing to take a week-long retreat during this time, we all still have work, family, relationships, and more that need us. Take a look at your calendar for the next week. What pockets of time can you find to rest? Block those times out and treat them as you would an important appointment. Don't cancel on yourself!

- Choose one or two items off the Self-Care Checklist on page 121 to try this week. Journal how you feel before and after.

- Journaling around the stories you carry that are not your own is so important. Take time this week to think about where your beliefs around rest actually come from (i.e., parents, school, religion). Use "Uncovering Should" on page 84 to help with this.

- Take a break from screens and digital devices to give your mind a rest from constant stimulation. Instead, indulge in activities, such as reading, going for a walk (without earbuds!), or journaling by hand.

- Guilt-free resting takes practice. Be kind to yourself.

In the moon's ebb and flow,
I find rest for my
weary soul

How can I trust in the process of letting go during this phase?

Consider moments when rest felt like an act of rebellion against societal norms. How did I feel to reclaim rest as a form of resistance?

How have my family's views on rest influenced my relationship with downtime? Are there generational patterns around rest I'd like to reshape?

If societal norms didn't dictate my approach to rest, how would I design my ideal restful practice? Consider activities, spaces, or rituals that genuinely nurture your need for rest.

Waning Crescent Moon Notes

WANING CRESCENT MOON
SPELLS & RITUALS

These spells are designed to help nurture your need for rest and reflection, fostering a peaceful space for rejuvenation and renewal. The Waning Crescent phase supports the gentle cocooning of your energy, allowing you to rest deeply and prepare for the next cycle of growth and action.

EMOTIONAL ALCHEMY SPELL

spell purpose: emotional release

when to cast: any time   **ritual time:** 15-20 minutes

ingredients: clear quartz, pen and paper, white candle

HOW TO PERFORM:

- **Center Yourself:** Take a few deep breaths, grounding yourself in the present moment. Light the white candle, representing purity and clarity. Hold the clear quartz crystal in your hands, feeling its energy and envisioning a sense of emotional balance and harmony.
- **Identify Your Emotion:** Look at the Emotional Guidance Scale (page 154) and name the emotion you're currently experiencing. Write it down in your journal.
- **Accept and Take Ownership:** Acknowledge and accept the emotion without judgment. Recognize its validity and your ownership of this feeling.
- **Embrace the Emotion:** Dive into the emotion fully, expressing it through speaking or writing in your journal.
- **Release:** Vent and process the emotion within the pages of your journal or through movement, allowing yourself to release it thoroughly.
- **Ascend:** Gradually climb the emotional scale, moving to the next resonating emotion. Ascend one or two steps at a time, honoring each feeling and delving into their depths without interference or judgement.
- **Avoid Rushing:** Resist the urge to rush or dismiss emotions prematurely. Respect each feeling's significance and depth.
- **Close and Express Gratitude:** There is no right or wrong time to complete this spell. You may wish to move up one or two emotions or five or six. Once you feel you are finished, thank the crystal for its assistance in this emotional ascension. Blow out the candle, symbolizing the completion of this transformative spell.

GUILT RELEASE SPELL

spell purpose: to embrace and honor the need for self-nurturing activities

when to cast: the Waning Moon   **ritual time:** 15-20 minutes

ingredients: lavender incense or dried lavender (calming and relaxing, aids in soothing the mind and releasing tension), black tourmaline crystal (powerful grounding stone, helps in dispelling negative energy and promoting feelings of security and protection), white candle (promotes purity, clarity, healing, amplifies positive energy, illuminating the space with pure intentions)

HOW TO PERFORM:

- **Create Sacred Space:** Light the white candle in a quiet area where you feel relaxed and at peace.
- **Set the Scene:** Light the lavender incense or place the dried lavender nearby to infuse the space with calming energy, preparing the atmosphere for relaxation and letting go.
- **Hold the Crystal:** Hold the black tourmaline crystal in your hand, feeling its grounding and protective energy. Its purpose is to assist in shedding feelings of guilt and fostering a sense of security during this ritual.
- **Let Go of Guilt:** Close your eyes and identify any guilt or weight you feel that's associated with taking rest. Then, take a deep breath and as you exhale, visualize the guilt leaving your body. The combined effect of the crystal, candle, and lavender helps facilitate this emotional release.
- **Affirm:** Whisper softly or think quietly, "I release guilt, embracing rest as a necessary act of self-care. My well-being matters." The spoken affirmation strengthens your intention to let go of guilt and prioritize self-care.
- **Call in Healing Energy:** Place the black tourmaline near the candle flame, allowing its protective energy to envelop the space and anchor your affirmation. The crystal helps in maintaining a protective and healing energy field around you.
- **Sit in Peace:** Sit quietly, feeling the peaceful energy of the space and affirmations. Allow the candle and incense to burn completely or extinguish them with a sense of tranquility once you feel the release has occurred.

RESTORATIVE DEEP REST SPELL

spell purpose: support deep rest and renewal, so you can recharge fully for the next cycle of growth.

when to cast: the Waning Crescent **ritual time:** 20-30 minutes

ingredients: soft blanket, white candle, piece of amethyst or moonstone, bowl of water with a pinch of sea salt, journal and pen

HOW TO PERFORM:

- **Create Your Space:** Find a quiet, comfortable place where you can be undisturbed and wrap yourself in a warm cocoon with the blanket.
- **Light the Candle:** Place the candle in front of you, and take a few deep breaths, inhaling peace and exhaling any lingering stress or tension.
- **Hold the Crystal**: Take the amethyst or moonstone in your hand, feeling its calming energy. Close your eyes and envision the Waning Crescent moon above, its soft light enveloping you in a soothing glow.
- **Reflect and Release:** As you sit in this peaceful space, think about any stress, obligations, or worries that have been weighing on you as shadows being gently drawn away by the moon's subtle glow, leaving you feeling lighter and more at ease.
- **Water Ritual:** Dip your fingers into the bowl of water, symbolically washing away any remaining tension or overwhelm. As you do, softly speak the words:

  > "In this moment, I release and renew,
  > In this moment, I find peace and what's true."

- **Journal**: When ready, open your journal and write down any thoughts, reflections, or intentions. You might note what you're releasing and how you want to feel as you enter the next phase.
- **Close the Ritual:** Gently blow out the candle, thanking the moon for its guidance. Take a moment to sit in silence, feeling the peaceful energy you've cultivated. When you're ready, wrap yourself more snugly in your blanket and rest.

CELEBRATING CYCLES

This planner is designed to help you celebrate the completion of your goal—no matter how many moon cycles it took. Use this space to plan a meaningful and joyous ritual that honors your progress, dedication, and the magical journey you've undertaken. Taking time to celebrate breaks us from the habit of constantly moving on to produce. It gives us the time and space to reflect and enjoy our lives.

chapter eight

CELEBRATION

ritual planner

LET'S CELEBRATE

This Celebration Ritual Planner is your guide to curating a personalized and meaningful ceremony that honors and amplifies the joy of your achievements. Whether big or small, every success deserves to be acknowledged with intention. Follow these steps to create a celebration that resonates with you. Goals often take longer to achieve when you are living in cycle with your body and the moon. This is why it is so important— *when you take the time to enjoy each stage, you aren't burned out in the end and can enjoy your success!*

Step 1: Reflect on Your Achievements

Before diving into the planning, use the follow pages "A Deep Dive into Your Journey" on page 134 and "Celebrating Your Unique Brilliance" on page 136 to reflect on your achievements. This reflection is an important step that will help you tailor your celebration to your unique journey.

Step 2: Choose a Setting, Date, and Time

Select a setting that holds significance for you. It could be in the comfort of your home, a serene outdoor space, or a venue that has personal importance. The environment should enhance the mood of celebration and relaxation. Choose a date and time that allows you to fully immerse yourself in the celebration. It could be on the actual achievement day or a designated day shortly after (within a two week time span.)

Step 3: Select a Theme or Mood

Consider incorporating a theme or mood that resonates with your achievements. It could be elegant, cozy, festive, or reflective. Choose something that captures the essence of your success and sets the tone for the celebration. Pinterest is a great tool for inspiration!

Step 4: Create Personalized Invitations

Even if it's a celebration just for yourself, create personalized invitations. This could be a handwritten note to yourself or a beautifully designed digital invitation. Capture the excitement and significance of the upcoming celebration.

Step 5: Plan the Menu

If your celebration involves a meal, plan a menu that includes your favorite dishes or those with special significance. Whether it's cooking a gourmet meal, ordering from your favorite restaurant, or preparing a ritual tea, let the food be a delightful part of the celebration.

Step 6: Incorporate Rituals and Ceremonies

Incorporate rituals or ceremonies that hold personal meaning. This could be lighting candles, expressing gratitude, or performing a symbolic gesture. Consider including elements that align with your achievements, creating a connection between the ritual and your success.

Step 7: Select a Playlist

Craft a playlist that complements the mood of your celebration. Include music that resonates with your achievements, brings back joyful memories, or simply makes you feel good. Music has the power to enhance the atmosphere and create a memorable experience.

Step 8: Capture the Moment

Whether through photographs, journaling, or creating art, find a way to capture the moment. This documentation serves as a tangible reminder of your achievements and that you made time to celebrate yourself and your life.

Step 9: Practice Gratitude and Reflection

End your celebration with a moment of gratitude and reflection. Express thanks for the journey, the support received, and the personal growth achieved. This closing ritual allows you to transition from the celebration with a sense of fulfillment.

Step 10: Share the Joy (Optional)

If comfortable, share the joy with friends or loved ones. This could be through a virtual gathering, a phone call, or a simple message. Sharing your achievements with others amplifies the joy and creates a sense of collective celebration.

A DEEP DIVE INTO YOUR JOURNEY

Take a moment to breathe and carefully consider the following prompts, guiding you through an examination of your achievements, challenges, and unexpected lessons. Use this reflection page as an opportunity to explore the nuances of your journey, acknowledging both the challenges and triumphs that have contributed to your growth.

Significant Milestones:
Reflect on the peaks of your journey. What were the moments that stood out? Consider not only the big accomplishments but also the smaller victories.

Challenges Overcome:
Acknowledge the challenges that you faced during this goal. What hurdles did you encounter, and how did you navigate through them? Recognize your resilience and resourcefulness in overcoming obstacles.

Unexpected Lessons Learned:
What surprising insights did you gain during your journey? These could be about yourself, your goals, or the world around you.

Moments of Growth:
Consider how you've grown personally and professionally. In what ways have you expanded your skills, mindset, or understanding of yourself? Growth is not always visible in the moment, so reflect on the subtle transformations that have taken place.

Proud Achievements:
Expressing pride in your achievements is a powerful way to reinforce a positive mindset. What have you learned and accomplished that makes you proud?

Surpassing Expectations:
Were there moments when you surprised yourself by surpassing your own expectations? Reflect on instances where you demonstrated capabilities or strengths you may not have fully recognized before.

Positive Habits Formed:
Reflect on any positive habits or routines that you established during this journey. Recognize the habits that contribute to your well-being.

Moment of Gratitude:
What aspects of your journey are you thankful for? Expressing gratitude can enhance your overall sense of accomplishment and satisfaction.

DEAR FUTURE SELF

Complete your celebration by writing a letter to your future self. Save this letter for when you are about to start a new journey or goal that feels intimidating. Use the prompts below to write a letter to remind yourself of what you are able to accomplish and things you learned about trusting yourself, the Universe, and nature's cycles. Let this letter serve as a reminder when you find yourself overwhelmed with fear.

Dear Future Self,

** Use these prompts to finish the letter**

Write Words of Encouragement: Write words of encouragement to your future self. Remind yourself of your strengths, resilience, and the unique qualities that set you apart. Let these words be a beacon of positivity to guide you through challenges and celebrate triumphs.

Trust in Your Own Abilities: Reaffirm your trust in your capabilities. Acknowledge the skills, talents, and strengths that have carried you through previous endeavors.

Identify Relationships and Connections: Reflect on the impact of your connections during your journey, recognizing the value of shared experiences and support.

Recognize the Power of Self-Trust: Reflect on moments when trusting yourself led to positive outcomes.

Reconnect with Your Inner Strength: During fearful or overwhelming moments, recall the times when you faced uncertainty and emerged stronger.

CELEBRATING YOUR UNIQUE BRILLIANCE

This self-appreciation exercise is designed to help you not only recognize but also celebrate your strengths and unique qualities that have played a pivotal role in your success.

Step 1: Identifying Strengths

Begin by reflecting on the strengths that have gotten you here today. These strengths are the pillars of your character and capabilities. Answer the following questions:

- What skills or talents do you possess that have been instrumental in your achievements?
- In what areas have you consistently excelled, and what personal qualities have contributed to this success?
- Think of moments when you felt empowered and confident. What strengths were at the forefront during those times?

Step 2: Acknowledging Achievements

Now, connect your strengths to specific achievements. Reflect on the goals you've accomplished and the times you've surpassed your own expectations.

- How did your strengths contribute to your successes?
- Were there instances where a particular strength shone brightly, leading you through challenges?
- Reflect on the positive impact your strengths have had on your journey.

Step 3: Celebrating Uniqueness

Every woman possesses unique qualities that makes her special. Take a moment to celebrate and acknowledge these aspects of yourself:

- What unique qualities do you bring to the table that set you apart from others?
- How have your unique perspectives or approaches contributed to your success?
- Consider the qualities that others admire or appreciate in you.

Step 4: Reflecting and Committing

- Take a moment to reflect: How did it feel to consciously acknowledge and celebrate your strengths?
- Consider the impact this self-awareness can have on your future endeavors.

Enjoy the journey,
so you can enjoy
the destination

A FOUR-WEEK JOURNEY

Create a personalized daily ritual to support your goals. Over the course of four weeks or one moon cycle, you'll gradually build a daily ritual, adding new elements each week to enhance your practice and align with your intentions. Discover the power of a daily practice to guide you on your path to success.

chapter nine

DAILY RITUAL

one step at a time

LET'S DO A LITTLE DAYDREAMING

One of the smallest, yet most powerful, things you can do to bring your dreams to life with ease is taking five minutes each day and daydreaming about what it will look and feel like to have that goal become a reality.

Visualizing your goal and savoring the emotions it brings not only enhances your current reality, but it also creates a magnetic field around you, drawing similar energies into your life. This process is a form of prayer, meditation, and spell work all in one—focusing your energy and co-creating with the Universe. **Remember, the energy you put out will match what you attract.**

In these moments of daily visualization, you are setting the stage for your goals to manifest **with ease**. The consistent practice helps you stay centered, focused, and motivated, making the journey a natural and enjoyable process. As you embrace this practice, you'll find that your goals are not just distant dreams but *living realities* that are steadily coming to fruition, guided by the beautiful energy you've cultivated within yourself.

I know it can be daunting to think about sitting with your goals and visualizing them, especially if you're afraid of not getting it right from the start or if you think, "I know I will miss days, so why even try?" Or it might feel like you should be jumping to more "important" tasks, worrying that if you don't succeed immediately, it's a sign to give up. But here's the truth: allowing yourself to be a beginner, not to expect perfection but to anticipate needing to restart is actually one of the most valuable things you can do for yourself. This is the nature of growth! It's natural and normal to stumble and to need time to learn. This is being human.

Every cycle, whether it's a New Moon or a new week, is an opportunity to start fresh and realign with your intentions. You're building a foundation, and that takes time and patience. **Allow yourself the space to try, to fail, and to begin again.**

So set a daily reminder, take five minutes and give yourself permission to enjoy this, knowing that every step you take, no matter how uncertain, is bringing you closer to your dreams. Trust that each cycle s a new chance to grow and evolve.

With each new beginning, you're building a life that aligns with your deepest desires, and that's worth every moment of effort.

WEEK ONE

Light, Breath, Feel

this daily ritual can take as little as 2-3 minutes
the key is consistency, not length

- **Light:** Light your candle and take a deep breath to center yourself.

- **Breathe:** Take a deep breath, feeling the air fill your lungs, and exhale slowly, allowing any tension to melt away.

- **Feel**: Close your eyes and visualize the feelings associated with achieving your goal. Feel the emotions as if they are already present in your life.

- **Complete**: After three to four breaths, blow out the candle gently, signifying the completion.

How did it feel?

WEEK TWO

Light, Breathe, Feel, Speak

*this daily ritual can take as little as 4-5 minutes
the key is consistency, not length*

- **Light:** Light your candle and take a deep breath to center yourself.

- **Breathe**: Take slow, deliberate breaths, allowing your body to relax and your mind to focus.

- **Feel**: Close your eyes and visualize the feelings associated with achieving your goal. Feel the emotions as if they are already present in your life.

- **Speak**: Speak this new truth aloud in a firm, confident tone. Let your voice and the power it holds fill the space around you.

- **Complete**: Gently blow out the candle, symbolizing the integration of this truth. Take a moment to reflect on how you feel after your ritual.

How did it feel?

WEEK THREE

Light, Breathe, Feel, Speak, Reflect

this daily ritual can take as little as 5-6 minutes
the key is consistency, not length

- **Light:** Light your candle and take a deep breath to center yourself.
- **Breathe:** Inhale deeply, filling your lungs, and exhale, releasing any tension or distractions.
- **Feel**: Close your eyes and visualize the feelings associated with achieving your goal. Feel the emotions as if they are already present in your life.
- **Speak**: Speak this new truth aloud in a firm, confident tone. Let your voice and the power it holds fill the space around you
- **Reflect:** Reflect on your day and identify three feeling words that you are currently feeling. No need to judge or change the emotions. Just allow this practice to deepen your emotional awareness. Write these words down in your journal.
- **Complete:** As you extinguish the candle, envision the integration of these feelings. Allow this practice to deepen your emotional awareness.

How did it feel?

WEEK FOUR

Light, Breathe, Feel, Speak, Reflect, Release

this daily ritual can take as little as 10 minutes
the key is consistency, not length

- **Light:** Light your candle and take a deep breath to center yourself.
- **Breathe:** Take a deep breath, feeling the air fill your lungs, and exhale slowly, allowing any tension to melt away.
- **Feel**: Close your eyes and visualize the feelings associated with achieving your goal. Feel the emotions as if they are already present in your life.
- **Speak**: Speak this new truth aloud in a firm, confident tone. Let your voice and the power it holds fill the space around you.
- **Reflect**: Reflect on your day and identify three feeling words that you are currently feeling. Write these words down in your journal.
- **Release:** Connect with your body through gentle movement. Let yourself express emotions through dance, stretching, or deliberate motions. Let the emotions flow freely through your body.
- **Complete**: As you blow out the candle, visualize the emotions flowing out of your body and a renewed sense of balance within you. Embrace the feeling of emotional liberation.

How did it feel?

Everyday is
a new beginning

DIVE DEEPER INTO MAGIC

There is always so much to learn about the magic in ourselves and nature. Here are a few resources to spark your curiosity and help you on your journey!

chapter ten

BONUS
RESOURCES

dive deeper

HERBS & THEIR MAGICAL USES

Lavender
- Purpose: Represents peace, purification, and tranquility.
- Uses: Used in spells for calming, relaxation, sleep, and cleansing rituals.

Rosemary
- Purpose: Symbolizes protection, clarity, and memory.
- Uses: Utilized in spells for protection, purification, and enhancing mental faculties.

Mugwort
- Purpose: Enhances psychic abilities and is a powerful protector.
- Uses: Used in spells for astral projection, lucid dreaming, and when protection is needed.

Thyme
- Purpose: Represents courage, strength, and purification.
- Uses: Used in spells for gaining courage, banishing negative energies, and enhancing vitality.

Cinnamon
- Purpose: Represents power, prosperity, and passion.
- Uses: Used in spells for boosting energy, attracting wealth, and igniting passion.

Basil
- Purpose: Symbolizes love, prosperity, and protection.
- Uses: Utilized in spells for attracting love, gaining wealth, and offering protection.

Bay Leaf
- Purpose: Represents manifestation, protection, and wishes.
- Uses: Used in spells for manifestation, protection, and actualizing desires.

148

DIFFERENT TYPES OF WITCHES

These are just a few examples of the diverse spectrum of witches. Many witches may identify with more than one type or incorporate elements from various traditions into their practice. The beauty of witchcraft lies in its flexibility, adaptability, and the personal connection each woman cultivates with her craft.

Green Witch: Deeply connected to nature and Earth. Specializes in herbalism and plant magic and often works with crystals and the moon. Practices revolve around fostering harmony with the natural world.

Energy Witch: Skilled in moving between the boundaries of the physical and spiritual realms. Often works with Reiki and is adept at divination and spirit communication.

Kitchen Witch: Finds magic in everyday activities, particularly in the kitchen. Infuses cooking and baking with intention, using herbs and spices for both magical and culinary purposes. The hearth is their sacred space.

Eclectic Witch: Draws inspiration from various traditions, creating a personalized and fluid practice. May incorporate elements from different cultures, belief systems, and magical techniques that resonate with them.

Moon Witch: Focuses their magic on the phases of the moon. Aligns their rituals and spellwork with the lunar cycles, drawing on the energy of the New Moon for beginnings, the Full Moon for power, and the waning moon for banishing.

Art Witch: Infuses their magical practice into their artistic expressions. May create spell-infused artwork, use art as a form of meditation, or incorporate artistic symbolism into their rituals.

Cosmic Witch: Works with celestial energies, including planets, stars, and cosmic forces. May align their magical workings with astrological events and planetary transits.

COLOR MAGIC

Colors hold vibrational energies that can influence spells and rituals in witchcraft. Each color carries specific symbolism and associations, enhancing the intention of magical workings.

RED — Passion, vitality, courage, and energy. It's used for spells related to love, strength, and vitality.

ORANGE — Creativity, success, and enthusiasm. It's utilized for spells related to ambition, creativity, and attraction.

YELLOW — Intellect, clarity, and communication. It's used for spells related to mental clarity, confidence, and optimism.

GREEN — Growth, abundance, and healing. It's used for spells related to fertility, prosperity, and health.

BLUE — Tranquility, wisdom, and intuition. It's utilized for spells related to healing, peace, and spiritual guidance.

PURPLE — Spirituality, intuition, and higher knowledge. It's used for spells related to psychic abilities, divination, and spiritual growth.

BLACK — Protection, banishing, and absorbing negativity. It's used for spells related to protection and expelling negative energies.

WHITE — Purity, cleansing, and spirituality. It's used for spells related to purification, new beginnings, and clarity.

CRYSTALS & THEIR MAGICAL USES

Amethyst
- Purpose: Spiritual protection, intuition, clarity, and calmness.
- Uses: Enhances meditation, promotes psychic abilities, aids in dream recall, and wards off negative energies.

Clear Quartz
- Purpose: Amplification of intentions, mental clarity, and energy purification.
- Uses: Charges other crystals, increases focus during rituals, and amplifies the effectiveness of spells.

Rose Quartz
- Purpose: Love, compassion, emotional healing, and self-love.
- Uses: Attracts love and positive relationships, aids in emotional healing, and promotes self-acceptance.

Citrine
- Purpose: Abundance, prosperity, joy, and creativity.
- Uses: Attracts wealth and success, encourages creativity, and brings forth positive energy.

Black Tourmaline
- Purpose: Protection, grounding, and repelling negative energies.
- Uses: Shields against negative influences, purifies energy, and provides a protective barrier.

Moonstone
- Purpose: Intuition, new beginnings, feminine energy, and emotional balance.
- Uses: Enhances intuition, connects with lunar energies, and aids in emotional healing.

Labradorite
- Purpose: Transformation, intuition, and spiritual awakening.
- Uses: Stimulates psychic abilities, encourages spiritual growth, and provides support during times of change and transformation.

151

MOON PHASE HERBAL TEA RITUALS

New Moon
Creating

- **Herbal Tea:** Chamomile
- **Energetic Properties:** Calming, soothing, introspective
- **Ritual/Intention:** Stir the tea in a clockwise direction, infusing it with your intentions. As you sip the tea, breathe in deeply, drawing in the energy of new beginnings.

Waxing Crescent
Setting Intentions

- **Herbal Tea:** Peppermint
- **Energetic Properties:** Energizing, uplifting, clarity-inducing
- **Ritual/Intention:** While preparing the tea, gently blow over the cup to infuse it with your intentions. As you drink it, repeat your affirmations aloud, empowering them with your voice.

First Quarter
Taking Action

- **Herbal Tea Blend:** Ginger, Turmeric, Lemon
- **Energetic Properties:** Invigoration, determination, action
- **Ritual/Intention:** While the tea steeps, add a slice of fresh lemon and stir the tea clockwise. As you sip, visualize yourself taking confident steps toward your goals. Embrace the energy of determination.

Waxing Gibbous
Reflecting and Adjusting

- **Herbal Tea:** Lemon Balm
- **Energetic Properties:** Balancing, centering, calming
- **Ritual/Intention:** As tea steeps, softly hum or chant, using sound to center your thoughts. Take deep breaths while sipping, allowing each exhale to release any tension. Reflecting on your progress, make necessary adjustments with a calm mind.

MOON PHASE HERBAL TEA RITUALS

Full Moon
Celebrating and Releasing

- **Herbal Tea:** Lavender
- **Energetic Properties:** Relaxing, soothing, releasing
- **Ritual/Intention:** While brewing the tea, stir it in a figure-eight motion, symbolizing the union of celebration and release.

Waning Gibbous
Practicing Gratitude

- **Herbal Tea:** Lavender
- **Energetic Properties:** Relaxing, soothing, releasing
- **Ritual/Intention:** Before sipping the tea, take a few moments to hold the cup in your hands and express gratitude for what you've achieved. Sip slowly, focusing on how gratitude feels in your body.

Last Quarter
Letting Go

- **Herbal Tea:** Valerian Root
- **Energetic Properties:** Grounding, calming, letting go
- **Ritual/Intention:** As the tea steeps, stir it counterclockwise, symbolizing the release of what no longer serves you. Drink the tea mindfully, imagining yourself releasing burdens with each sip.

Waning Crescent
Resting and Recharging

- **Herbal Tea:** Passionflower
- **Energetic Properties:** Relaxing, restorative, introspective
- **Ritual/Intention:** While preparing the tea, infuse it with gentle stirring motions, envisioning the herbs releasing their calming properties. As you drink, focus on your breath, allowing it to relax you.

EMOTIONAL GUIDANCE SCALE

Using this scale can help you identify your current emotional state and work toward improving your feelings. By acknowledging where you are, you can use specific affirmations to help you accept and release these emotions, allowing yourself to gradually move upward.

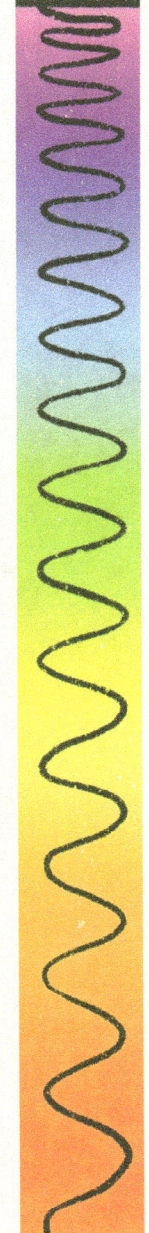

- **Joy/Love/Appreciation:** "I am a beacon of love and light."
- **Passion:** "My passion fuels my purpose, guiding me forward."
- **Enthusiasm/Eagerness/Happiness:** "I welcome joy into every facet of my life."
- **Positive Expectation/Belief:** "My belief in myself shapes my reality."
- **Optimism:** "My future is filled with limitless possibilities."
- **Hopefulness:** "The sun shines beyond these clouds; hope guides me through the dark.
- **Contentment:** "I am content in the present, grateful for my journey."

- **Boredom:** "I seek inspiration and uncover excitement in the ordinary."
- **Pessimism:** "I choose to see challenges as opportunities for growth."
- **Frustration/Irritation:** "I am patient and in control of my breathing and reactions."
- **Overwhelm:** "I breathe in peace, exhale chaos. I handle challenges with grace and ease."
- **Disappointment:** "Disappointment teaches; I find lessons in its whispers."
- **Doubt:** "I acknowledge doubt but embrace unwavering trust in my abilities and my path."
- **Anxiety/Worry:** "I let go of worry, come back to now, and trust in the unfolding of life."
- **Blame:** "I empower myself by taking responsibility for my life."
- **Discouragement:** "I persist despite discouragement, knowing I'm capable."
- **Anger:** "I alchemize anger into powerful, positive action."
- **Revenge:** "Revenge will not bring justice; I seek peace and understanding."
- **Hatred/Rage:** "Forgiveness liberates me, releasing the hold of rage."
- **Jealousy:** "No one walks my path, and in this truth, I celebrate others' success."
- **Insecurity/Guilt/Unworthiness/Shame:** "I am whole and worthy of love, forgiveness, and self-compassion."
- **Fear/Grief/Depression/Despair/Powerlessness:** "I am not defined by fear; I am resilient, capable of healing and renewal."

FEELINGS WHEEL

ADDITIONAL READING & RESOURCES

These resources offer valuable insights and have taught me so much. Please note that I do not fully endorse all the views or practices presented in these materials. I encourage you to take only what resonates with you on your personal journey. As always, trust your intuition and choose what aligns with your values and beliefs.

COMING SOON!
Moon Magic Planner: *A Lunar Planner for Achieving Goals Without Burnout*
by Melissa Lyon West *(Coming Spring 2025)*

Atomic Habits: *An Easy & Proven Way to Build Good Habits & Break Bad Ones*
by James Clear
*Clear's method for building habits has helped me understand how to create sustainable routines. If you want a practical approach to aligning habits with your lunar intentions, *Atomic Habits* provides valuable insights for lasting change.

Burnout: *The Secret to Unlocking the Stress Cycle*
by Emily Nagoski, PhD, and Amelia Nagoski, DMA
*This book transformed my understanding of stress, especially the importance of completing the stress cycle to avoid burnout. I highly recommend you move this to the top of your reading pile!

The Green Witch: *Your Complete Guide to the Natural Magic of Herbs, Flowers, Essential Oils, and More*
by Arin Murphy-Hiscock
*This guide connects beautifully with the magic of nature that I emphasize in *Moon Magic*. It offers practical knowledge on herbs and natural remedies, making it perfect for those looking to deepen their connection with nature while working on goals.

The Moon: *Calendar Moon Phases App*
developed by: Vitalii Gryniuk
*This app has been an essential tool in helping me stay attuned to the moon's cycles. It is a convenient way to track moon phases.

Rest Is Resistance: *A Manifesto*
by Tricia Hersey
*Hersey's message that rest is a birthright, not something to be earned, deeply shifted my perspective. Her insights on rest as essential to growth and well-being perfectly complement the lunar cycles of renewal and reflection.

Never forget, you are magic

THANK YOU

Dear Magical Reader,

Thank you for giving this book a chance.

If you enjoyed *Moon Magic* and found it helpful, the best way to show your support is by leaving a five-star review. It really helps other readers find the book and spreads the magic even further.

Thank you for your support and for being part of this magical journey!

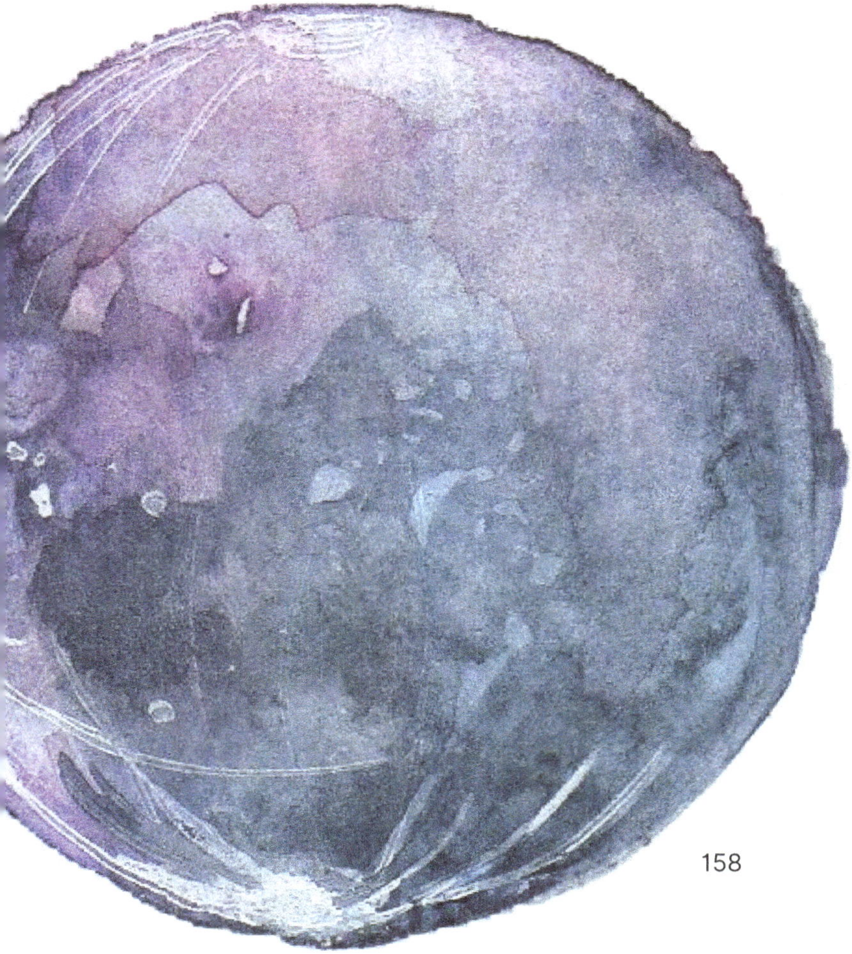

Scan to leave a review

ACKNOWLEDGMENT

First and foremost, I want to express my deepest gratitude to my beautiful and grounded partner, Robert. Thank you for always believing in me and my wild, often endless ideas, especially during moments when I started to doubt. Your unwavering support and steady presence have been my rock, allowing my creativity to flourish without spinning out of control. I couldn't have, and wouldn't have, done this without you.

To my incredible kids, Arrabella, Cecelia, Charlotte, and Silas, your endless encouragement, understanding when I would spend the day hidden away at the library, and enthusiastic requests for a signed copy kept me going. Your belief in me means the world, and I hope this book inspires you as much as you inspire me.

To Angelique Fish, my incredible friend and editor, whose steady belief in me has been a source of constant inspiration and encouragement since I met you in the desert four years ago. Your dedication to empowering women shines through in everything you do, and your support has been instrumental in bringing this book to life.

To Breea, my sister from another mister, when soon after meeting, you handed me that titty crystal I should have know it would be a wild ride with you. You have made this book infinitely better with your insight and ideas. Brainstorming with you is pure magic.

To Bree, Katrina, Rahdika, and Sheila: the women that inspired me during this journey, thank you. Your vulnerably and bravery motivated me to push forward and bring this book to life.

Thank you all for being a part of this magical journey.

You don't have to do this alone.

The Coaching Coven is a supportive group experience for ambitious women seeking creativity, rest, magic, and ease in their lives while achieving goals.

Find community and personalized coaching to apply what you learned in *Moon Magic* to your unique life goals. Stay accountable and motivated, and gain access to exclusive resources that will expand your knowledge and experience.

This community is a haven for those who are weary of the hustle and ready to achieve their dreams with joy and ease.

Scan to learn more

ABOUT THE AUTHOR

Born into a fundamentalist cult, Melissa found solace and safety in nature from a young age. She would lose herself in the woods for hours, creating potions and exploring the forest, finding both refuge and enchantment.

After breaking free, Melissa channeled her teaching experience and a decade of lessons from deconstructing and rebuilding an entire life and belief system into helping women connect with their innate power. Drawing from personal experiences of relentless ambition and subsequent burnout, Melissa discovered an alternative path beyond the constraints of what the patriarchy, white supremacy, and capitalism have taught. Embracing the cyclical wisdom of nature, she found a balance that brought rest and rejuvenation through witchcraft.

A passionate hiker and adventurer, Melissa loves spending time in the mountains of Utah but also enjoys lazy days in the hammock with a good novel or puttering in the garden. She loves swearing, comes alive when she throws elaborate dinner parties, thrives on deep conversations, and believes plant medicine saved her life.

She is a mom to four wild, beautiful children and a rescued doodle who is her constant shadow, and she creates this magical, chaotic life with her best friend and unbelievably supportive partner.

author photo by Becca Hofmann, BH Brand Co